Quilts of Indiana

Frontispiece: *Indiana Rose. Appliqued and pieced medallion quilt. Made by Anna Neukam Braun. Haysville, DuBois County, Indiana. Circa 1925. Cotton. 71½" × 66". Collection of Ruth Elkins.*

QUILTS

OF INDIANA

Crossroads of Memories

The Indiana Quilt Registry Project, Inc.

BOOK COMMITTEE CHAIRPERSONS

MARILYN GOLDMAN and MARGUERITE WIEBUSCH

BOOK COMMITTEE

Roxanne Fike
Karen Cochran Hasler
Mary Kay Horn
Anita Hawkins Krug
Kathleen McLary
Anne Scales
Cheryl A. Spence

Indiana University Press Bloomington and Indianapolis

**With the support of the
Indiana Arts Commission and
National Endowment for the Arts.**

The Indiana Quilt Registry Project received financial support from the Indiana Arts Commission and the National Endowment for the Arts.

The paper used in this publication meets the minimum requirements of American National Standard for Information Sciences—Permanence of Paper for Printed Library Materials, ANSI Z39.48-1984. ∞ ™

Printed in Singapore

Library of Congress Cataloging-in-Publication Data

Quilts of Indiana : crossroads of memories / the Indiana Quilt
   Registry Project, Inc. ; Book Committee chairpersons, Marilyn
Goldman and Marguerite Wiebusch ; Book Committee, Roxanne Fike . . .
[et al.]
       p.   cm.
   Includes bibliographical references and index.
   ISBN 0-253-32925-6 (acid-free paper). — ISBN 0-253-20644-8 (pbk.
   : acid-free paper)
   1. Quilts—Indiana—History.   I. Indiana Quilt Registry Project.
TT835.Q56   1991
746.9'7'09772—dc20   90-49157

1   2   3   4   5   95   94   93   92   91

CONTENTS

Preface

The women who stirred the kettle, rocked the cradle, and wielded the needle rarely merit mention in history books. This book aims to give recognition to these women. Although women have always practiced quilting—sometimes for pleasure, but often from necessity—not enough has been written about the lives of quilters and their art form. Quilters' art work didn't fit the mold. It wasn't painted, sculpted, or carved. It was rarely signed, so the makers by and large remained anonymous. What little history is available we have tried to present here, to preserve it for future generations.

Everybody will feel at home with the majority of the quilts (mostly made in Indiana by Indiana quiltmakers) in this book. They are familiar patterns—familiar from our childhood or from Grandma's trunk. A few are unusual. Some are outstanding, in particular the quilts designed by Marie Webster and those made by Susan McCord. We were indeed fortunate to be able to include these two historic quiltmakers in this volume. But all of the quilts, whether the pattern is familiar or not, are distinguished by creative touches that could only have been introduced by the individual who made them. Each one, in that sense, is special and unique. We have also been fortunate, in the case of many of these Indiana quilters, to be able to pass on in this volume the histories and photographs that were so kindly shared with us by their families.

The Indiana Quilt Registry Project, Inc. (IQRP), is a nonprofit corporation under the laws of the State of Indiana. It was formed in 1986 to actively engage in the documentation of quilts and quilters, both past and present. Its current goals include an exhibit of statewide findings, a publication, archives with public access, and public education about the care and preservation of quilts. The IQRP is headquartered at the Indiana State Museum, 202 North Alabama Street, Indianapolis, IN 46204, and is directed by a board of volunteers. The project is supported by public donations and through memberships and group sponsorships of registry days throughout the state of Indiana. Quilting groups, historical societies, and quilt shops, as well as interested individuals, participated. The Cummins Engine Company, the Indiana Arts Commission and the National Endowment for the Arts, the Indiana State Museum, and the National Quilting Association have been ardent supporters of IQRP's efforts.

Following the successful conclusion of quilt registry projects in other states, a similar endeavor was proposed for Indiana. In November 1986 an organizational meeting was held at which officers were elected.

The first phase of the project was the gathering of data from all over the state. This was done at the nineteen Registry Days held between April 1987 and April 1989. A list of registration sites is in the back of the book. Local groups co-sponsored the activity by underwriting the expenses and providing staff. Expenses for photography, hall and table rental, and publicity were financed from donations, raffles, bake sales, sales of "I Love Indiana Quilts" pins and magnets, and Indiana Rose applique block kits. In addition, some museums made quilts in their collections available for registration. These included the Indiana State Museum, William Hammond Mathers Museum of Indiana University, the Children's Museum of Indianapolis, Minnetrista Cultural Center, and county museums from Boone, Cass, Delaware, Henry, Jay, Johnson, Kosciusko, Monroe, Tippecanoe, and Wabash Counties. The Henry Ford Museum of Dearborn, Michigan, allowed board members to photograph and inspect the Susan McCord quilts housed there. The Indianapolis Museum of Art granted access to their collection of Marie Webster materials.

The second phase of the project was selection of quilts for the planned book and exhibit. IQRP board members completing the first phase and involved in the second were: Kathleen McLary, Anita Hawkins Krug, Marilyn Goldman, Cheryl A. Spence, Marguerite Wiebusch, Anne Scales, Roxanne Fike, Mary Kay Horn, and Karen Cochran Hasler. Because they moved out of the state, members Ellen Penwell and Millie Leathers completed Phase 1 but did not participate in Phase 2 and beyond. Documentation from each site was reviewed by at least three board members and quilts were singled out for possible inclusion in the book and/or exhibit on two merits—visual appeal and quilt history. Then the board again read the histories, reviewed the slides, and made an effort to choose the finalists to include as many Indiana counties of origin as possible.

From the 6,400 registered, the field was eventually narrowed to about 100 quilts, whose owners were then notified that the board wished to review their quilts. Some owners preferred that their quilts not be included, and some quilts were in such fragile condition that any additional handling would have been inadvisable.

Phase 3 is the publication, by Indiana University Press, of *Quilts of Indiana*, to coincide with Phase 4, an exhibit at the Indiana State Museum.

Phase 5 is establishment of an Archives at the Indiana State Museum. At the time of registration each quilt received its own archival number on a cloth tag, which we hope will remain with the quilt throughout the remainder of its existence. Photos of all quilts photographed are also in the Archives, which reside at the Indiana State Museum, 202 N. Alabama Street, Indianapolis, IN 46204. They are open to the public by appointment for the purpose of researching quilts and quilters.

In order to protect against fraud or theft, archival information does not include the names of current quilt owners. For similar reasons, quilt owners in this book are identified by name but not by address.

Quilts of Indiana gives a representative selection of the quilts found at registry sites and covers approximately two hundred years of quilt history. If more than a tiny portion of the quilts registered had been included here, the book would have been impossibly large and expensive.

Quilts of Indiana

Introduction: From *Cuilte* to Quilt

Quilts began in that dim prehistoric time when humans ceased hunting their clothing and started growing it. A sandwich of woven fabrics stuffed with wool, silk, or cotton padded ancient Chinese warriors and graced royal bedchambers. A medieval suit of armor was made bearable by quilted padding. Buildings which lacked central heating could be tolerated if one wore quilted petticoats or robes.

The need for adequate protection against rigorous climates prompted the use of quilted hangings for doors, windows, walls, and around the bed. The hangings on the bed would make it a room unto itself, able to contain body heat so that the occupants could sleep in relative comfort even in bone-chilling cold. It also afforded protection from flying insects, drafts, and other unpleasant elements of nature.

The history of quilting is closely tied to the development of other needle arts and home crafts. Spinning and weaving, and the invention of the loom, which has often been credited to China's Lady Si-Ling, wife of Emperor Huang-Ti in 2640 B.C., all made possible the later arts of dyeing, piecework, patchwork, and quilting as well as the closely related surface embellishment arts.

Ancient Egyptian textiles, as is evidenced in the cotton, linen, and woolen cloth found in the tombs of their kings, showed that these people were well versed in the use of mordants for dyeing and used embroidery extensively, although quilts were unknown in their warmer climate.

Tapestry and rug making existed as arts in the Middle East as early as two thousand years ago. Some patchwork from this time was crafted on regal robes and on canopies of leather used by nomadic Arabs. Bath or prayer rugs were often quilted in ancient Persia.

The English word "quilt" is derived from the Latin *culcitra*, which means a stuffed mattress or cushion, and the French word *cuilte*, *cotra*, or *coutre*, which evolved into "counterpoint" or "counterpane." The "pane" is from the Latin *pannus*, meaning a piece of cloth. A "counterpane" is a generic term for a quilt or coverlet.

By the Middle Ages, the church's need for vestments and robes served as an impetus for the development of needle arts, although quilting itself is not found in Western European cultures until after the Crusades. Quilted garments had been used for centuries by Eastern warriors and caught on quickly with the Crusaders, who used the padding to ease chafing from the heavy metal armor, absorb perspiration, and eliminate sores from allergies to the metals, as well as giving added protection from weapons. Cotton and silk were brought to Western Europe in the trade bonanza that followed these adventures. Appliqued hangings and garments from the Middle Eastern regions became the rage.

Quilting became popular in Europe in the eleventh century. The Moorish influence in Spain made that country among the first to excel in applique, the art of applying surface design to a background. One of the earliest recorded quilts was commissioned by the Queen of Portugal and was given as a wedding gift to her favorite lady in waiting. The quilt top had an embroidered design on closely quilted linen and was made by Portuguese monks who were missionaries in India.

Italian needlework techniques of the sixteenth century included embroidery and applique. An early Italian quilt, circa 1400, is described as buff-colored linen stitched in outline with brown thread and padded with wool. It shows battle scenes and is housed in London's Victoria and Albert Museum. Bits of floral scroll and lettering enhance the design.

French tents from the Middle Ages were frequently of leather patchwork, while early Northern European quilts were actually thick comforters filled with wool, feathers, or straw, like a mattress.

The value of these items was substantial among the rich and landed. Their estates listed clothing, bed coverings, and hangings, which were patched, appliqued, embroidered, and quilted. Dowries included quilts and bed clothing items. Queen Elizabeth I of England slept with ornate bed chamber hangings and a bed quilt.

Some early eighteenth century quilts were whole-cloth types, with no right or wrong side. The quilting itself may have been done in running stitch, back stitch, or chain stitch. These whole-cloth beauties depend entirely on stitching for the design or relief. Messages or mottoes might be stitched into the piece.

Applied work cut from colored cloth sewn in place with the buttonhole stitch has been a popular technique since the 1700s. Quilts of silk and satin fabrics that were found in France and Italy had been embroidered in gold and silver twist threads.

Quilting was introduced to the American colonies primarily by the English and Dutch. These two groups settled in the northern climates with their families, built homes, and practiced the household arts. Some quilted petticoats have survived from the colonial period, as have some chintz bed quilts. Since the Spanish journeyed to the warmer regions of the New World, they had no need of bed quilts there. The French, who explored into the far reaches of Canada, mostly utilized the hides they trapped, traded, and hunted for warmth.

American Indians for the most part bypassed the early quilts, going directly from skins and hides to traded blankets of wool and felted materials. Some Plains Indians adopted quilting later from the groups who settled and lived around them.

Before cloth was widely available in the American colonies, it had to be imported or saved from used clothing. Garment scraps were stitched into patchwork scrap quilts which have evolved as an American art form.

The invention of the cotton gin in 1793 insured the future of a textiles industry in the United States. The availability of raw materials, coupled with an expanding market, investment capital, and the establishment of factories, changed domestic textiles forever.

On plantations in the early southern colonies, looms wove wool, cotton, and flax fabrics for clothing and quilts. Having their own source of supply in raw cotton guaranteed that the first totally American-made cotton quilts were southern coverings. Indigo blue was the most common eighteenth century color because it was so permanent. An indigo dyepot was standard equipment in colonial homes.

The African fiber heritage can be seen in quilts made of strips which derive their inspiration from the narrow loom weavings done by the peoples of Africa. When translated into quilting and enhanced by use of available scrap materials, the ethnic look of Afro-American textiles was in distinct contrast to the European style that had developed as the Early American standard.

After the Revolution, a wave of primarily English settlers moved westward through the wilderness and across the Appalachian Mountains. Since they were isolated from imports, the women relied on basic techniques they had brought with them to grow, spin, weave, and dye their own fabrics.

When self-sufficiency failed, the women sought to trade or barter chickens, eggs, or skills for fabrics, particularly the colorfast, oil-dyed Turkey red cottons. Many quilts of the nineteenth century include this Turkey red cotton, usually accompanied by a home-dyed green that may have lost some of its dye and become yellowish, bluish, or even tan in color with age. Background fabrics from this period are almost always white.

When steamboat and rail transportation was established, fabrics for quilts and clothing could be imported to even the most remote of frontier areas.

The Industrial Revolution brought textile mills to the northern United States that utilized the cotton grown in the South. Having a non-imported source of fabric freed quilters everywhere from the constraints placed on them to scrimp, scrounge, and save scraps. Planned, formal quilts using the same fabrics throughout could be made from new fabrics. Following the War between the States, textile mills flourished in the south as well, encouraging development of diverse textiles.

The invention of the sewing machine (ca. 1850) with its many home uses prompted nineteenth-century quiltmakers to try piecing, appliqueing, and quilting on this new device.

This period also brought changes from hand production methods such as wood block printing and later copperplate printing to the use of silk screen and steel-roller printing and photoengraving for printing fabrics. Colors changed, too, as fabric dyeing evolved from a craft utilizing vegetable dyes to a chemical industry.

Early quilting designs were patterns of clam-shells, rainbows (later called the Baptist Fan), lines (single, double, or triple parallels), squares, and diamonds. More experienced quilters emulated ostrich plumes for complex curves and circles. Borders could contain fans or twisted rope patterns. Outlines of pieced and appliqued shapes are traditional and time-honored quilting techniques.

For women, social life on the frontier or in the rural areas was very limited. The quilting bee was a ritual of life. Group quilts were done of necessity and for gifts and dowries. The Ladies Aid Society of the local community church provided another social outlet for women, formalizing the togetherness of the quilting bee. Present-day quilt guilds are descended from these traditional forms of women's activities.

The local county fair competition was the forerunner of the quilt show and competition. The emphasis was heavy on craftsmanship and "stitches to the inch" rather than solely on design or originality. All the quilts were for bed use. A wall hanging was unheard of during this period of quilting.

Magazines and newspapers began to promote readership and communication in the quilt world by printing local or syndicated columns featuring patterns for pieced, appliqued, or embroidered blocks. This enhanced communication made it possible for a quilter in rural Medaryville, Indiana, to win an honorable mention in a quilt contest promoting the 1939 New York World's Fair.

In the twentieth century the development of synthetics has had an impact on the quilt world. Although some of these new fabrics are used in quilts, the staple is still cotton. However, when it comes to batting for the inside of the quilt, polyesters dominate while cotton batt is in the minority.

The twentieth century has also seen a widespread use of commercial patterns and kits available from clubs, magazines, stores, and newspapers. Although American quilts began their development lagging behind their European counterparts, innovations in quilting can be claimed. Seminars, conventions, and workshops are widely held in the United States and attract participants from all over the world. The art quilt has become a universal medium since gallery showings of quilts began in the early 1970s. Elevating the quilt from the bed to the wall has at last laid to rest the art-versus-craft argument. The historical importance of quilting has been enhanced by the widespread acceptance of search and research projects involving quilts and quilters in the United States in the last ten years. Television programs and videos on quilting are a world away from quilting by candle or oil lamp, or even by firelight.

It's been a long, fascinating journey from *cuilte* to quilt.

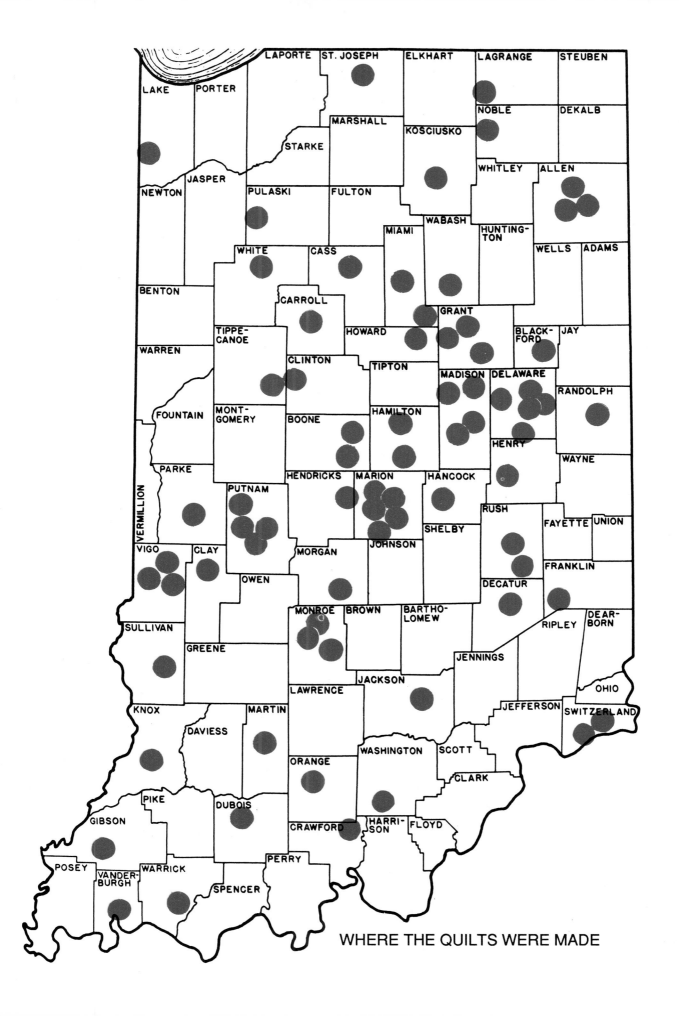

WHERE THE QUILTS WERE MADE

5

Frontier Folk Art

1 When the Ice Age subsided, the northern two-thirds of Indiana was as flat as a quilt top, while the southern third remained as rumpled as an unmade bed. Earth pillows nestled along the Ohio River. Prehistoric Indians called Mound Builders were the first people to live in the area. They were followed by the Miami Indians, who were residing in Indiana when the French began their explorations. As Indians lost their lands in the eastern United States, many other tribes moved into the area.

The beginnings of recorded history find French explorers, missionaries, and traders along the portages of the Maumee and Wabash Rivers in the Fort Wayne area, the Saint Joseph and Kankakee Rivers in the South Bend area, and the Ohio River in the Jeffersonville–New Albany area. French travelers established the first permanent settlement in Indiana at Vincennes in 1732.

French and British interests collided in the French and Indian War, 1754–1763. Failing in the war, the French were forced to cede their interests to Britain. Following its defeat in the Revolutionary War, Britain in turn ceded the entire region to the United States. What became known as the Northwest Territory was a vast tract of land lying north of the Ohio River, west of Pennsylvania, and east of the Mississippi River that extended northward to the Great Lakes.

In 1800 the Ohio Territory was separated from the Northwest Territory, and land west of Ohio became the Indiana Territory. It encompassed a large section of what is now the midwestern United States, including present-day Illinois, Indiana, Michigan, Wisconsin, and part of Minnesota. In this vast area, with its great stretches of virgin forest dotted with new fields full of tree stumps, lived 4,875 settlers, 2,517 of them in what later became Indiana.

President Thomas Jefferson sent William Henry Harrison, a Virginian, to govern the Indiana Territory, headquartered at Vincennes. He held the office until 1812. By that time the territory had been greatly reduced by the splitting off and creation of Michigan (1805) and Illinois (1809), the capital had been moved to Corydon, the population had increased fourhundredfold, and the first unsuccessful petition for statehood had been submitted to Congress.

Self-sufficiency was a necessity in such sparsely settled territory. To achieve it, life was a never-ending routine of grueling work. While the men cleared the land and farmed, women had the responsibility for maintaining house and garden, which meant not only chores like cooking, cleaning, washing, tending chickens, and churning butter but also making clothing for every individual in the household, often spinning the thread and weaving the cloth as well as assembling (and later mending) of the garment.

The earliest bed covering found during the registry was a blue glazed silk quilt stitched with burgundy thread. The quilting pattern resulted in a central medallion monogram. The most interesting aspect of the quilt was the batting, which consisted of a burlap-canvas construction. It turned out to be an Italian quilt, dating from about 1700, which had been brought to northern Indiana by twentieth-century immigrants.

Surviving quilts from the territorial period are of several distinctive types, and they tend to be functional, not ornamental. The fabrics most often used were wool, linen, cotton, and sometimes silk. There are whole-cloth quilts, broderie perse, blue-resist dyed, and pieced quilts of loom-woven natural materials.

Broderie perse is an early form of applique in which motifs from expensive chintz-printed fabrics were cut out and stitched onto a plain ground, usually unbleached muslin or linen. The top was then quilted heavily and bound, often with fringe, cording, or lace. Broderie perse appliques were frequently inspired by palampores, a type of cotton bedspread from India that was printed or painted. One popular motif was the Tree of Life design.

Resist dyeing is an eighteenth-century technique for indigo printing. A paste or wax mixture was used as a resist to protect areas of plain fabric that were not to be dyed, while the indigo dye was applied to the unprotected areas to produce the required design. Florence Pettit in *America's Printed and Painted Fabrics, 1600–1900* calls blue-resist fabrics "the most independently original and distinctive American printed fabrics of the New World's first 300 years."

Some of the whole-cloth quilts of this era were whitework with cording and stuffing, commonly called trapunto today. Other whole-cloth quilts were in glazed wools; these are sometimes called "linsey-woolsey," implying a mixture of linen and wool. More likely, the quilt will have one wool side and a cotton of coarse weave on the reverse.

Woven fabrics used in quilts may have been produced at home by the user of the fabric, in a cottage-industry situation resembling that in which coverlet weavers worked, or in factory-like settings. Some wood-block printed fabrics, engraved copperplate fabrics, and imported toiles also made their way to the Indiana frontier.

Indiana's quilting history appears to begin with whole-cloth and broderie perse quilts. The small number of broderie perse quilts registered indicates that although glazed chintz was available, this style was not widely made in Indiana. Family histories tell us that two of the three found were made in New England and later brought to Indiana. The fabrics were the dark hues typical of chintz, cut out, carefully arranged on a white ground cloth, and appliqued into a medallion and border motif.

The myth that early settlers began spinning and weaving, with looms on their laps, as they headed west was not substantiated by this project. Three handspun, pieced quilts, all from southwestern Indiana, showed the use of home-spun, home dyed, and home-woven fabric. Wool batting was used in each. All had at least a two-piece back constructed similarly to those found in early nineteenth-century Indiana coverlets. The back of one wool quilt consisted of fourteen separate pieces, a true scrap-pieced back!

Owing to the War of 1812, Indiana's 1810 statehood petition was not acted upon, so in 1815 a second petition was made. Population of the territory was by then 63,897. This time Congress reacted favorably; on April 19, 1816, an Enabling Act was passed and in the summer of 1816 a constitutional convention met at Corydon to draw up a state constitution. The first governor, thirty-two-year-old Jonathan Jennings, and the state's first General Assembly were elected in August, and on December 11, 1816, Indiana was admitted to the Union as the nineteenth state.

In that same year the seven-year-old Abraham Lincoln moved with his family from Kentucky to Spencer County in southwestern Indiana. There he remained until the age of twenty-one, during which time he received a total of less than twelve months of formal schooling—not untypical for the times.

Early settlers had used the Ohio River and Lake Michigan to reach their destinations in Indiana.

Eventually they had the National Road as well. This was a federal project beginning in Cumberland, Maryland in 1811 and slowly extending westward. In the 1830s it reached Indiana, crossing through the central section from Richmond through Indianapolis and Terre Haute. Although primitive—in places little more than a partially cleared trail—it was the main route westward, and an important means of local transportation as well. Today known as U.S. 40, the National Road extends from Washington, D.C., to Saint Louis.

In 1818 two-thirds of the land in the state was still in Indian hands. Land cession treaties and Indian removal culminated in 1838 under Governor David Wallace when troops under the leadership of General John Tipton forced the removal of 900 Potawatami Indians to Missouri in a badly organized march that brought sickness and death and came to be known as the Trail of Tears. The Miami Indians did not hold out much longer. By the mid-1850s few Indians were left in Indiana, and the pioneer era itself was over.

The early statehood-era quilts we found in Indiana were most frequently formal quadrant style or floral appliques. In the quadrant style the quilt top is divided visually into four sections. The sections may all be identical or each may be different. The four sections of the quadrant may be butted together to resemble the whole-cloth style of the previous decades, or the four sections may be divided by sashings. The sashings in turn can be coordinated solids or piecework. Borders for this style of quilt may feature solid fabrics or appliqued strips with swag designs. The beginnings of the quilt of nine block repeats date to this period.

Quilt colors were often red and green on a white background. Occasionally touches of antimony orange, pink, or chrome yellow gave additional sparkle. These were the stable colors women came to depend upon. Redyeing of clothes and other household textiles was a routine duty, but since there was no satisfactory way to redye an entire quilt and maintain a white background, the fabrics used had to be colorfast. Turkey red dyes, so called because they originated in the Middle East, were the quilters' salvation. The red madder dye was fixed to the fabric by an oil process and the fabric, though expensive, was very durable.

Applique quilts frequently featured flowers. The rose was a particular favorite; it was rendered in various forms—Rose of Sharon, Lancaster Rose, Ohio Rose, Indiana Rose, and Harrison Rose, among others. The Harrison Rose pattern was widely used following the death of President William Henry Harrison in 1841 shortly after his Inauguration. The War with Mexico brought Mexican Rose and Poinsettia motifs to women who stitched while men fought and governed.

Utility quilts of the period most frequently were simple geometric designs, bars or squares, either recycled from old suiting or newly loomed by the maker. Designed for comfort, warmth, and serviceability, they were usually in darker colors so that frequent laundering was not necessary.

Large stars were also a popular motif for quilts of this era, replacing the palampore Tree of Life designs of earlier years. Star patterns, large and small, were by far the most popular of all quilt designs found during the project regardless of the time frame. Large single star patterns like Star of Bethlehem or Lone Star have great visual appeal. They can be quite striking. The design also lends itself to additional patchwork or applique, perhaps folk art flowers and birds, in the large plain corner areas and triangles used to complete the quilt. Bar-type borders were sometimes used to frame the quilt.

Broderie Perse Medallion

Broderie perse medallion. Appliqued quilt. Maker and origin unknown. Circa 1800. Cotton chintz. 84½" × 82¾". Collection of the Indiana State Museum.

Literally the term broderie perse means Persian embroidery, but any type of early cut-out chintz applique qualifies for this category. Chintz is a glazed cotton, originally from India, but imitated widely. It was printed with large floral or natural images usually in five colors and was very expensive. With the broderie perse technique, a little of this expensive fabric could be made to go a long way.

Blue Resist Quilt

Whole-cloth indigo blue resist print. Made by Mrs. Eugene W. Crane. Haverford, Connecticut. Circa 1800.
Cotton. 96" × 86". Collection of the Children's Museum of Indianapolis.

Although this is a whole-cloth style quilt, the top consists of three pieces or strips of fabric joined together. It is possible that the strips were from older hangings. It is quilted in clamshell design.

Blue resist was a process used to create a pattern on cloth. A paste or wax resist was used to protect the fabric from the indigo dye and to keep the undyed areas white. The unprotected areas were dyed, creating the design desired.

The Tarkington Quilt

Pieced and appliqued quilt. Made by Martha Wood Stamson. Indianapolis, Marion County, Indiana. Circa 1800. Cotton. 88" × 87". Collection of the Children's Museum of Indianapolis.

The central medallion of the present quilt is an appliqued crib quilt to which a larger pieced top was added; the newly enlarged piece was quilted as one. The inked names of five generations of owners appear on the quilt: 1800—Martha Wood Stamson; 1831—Maria Stamson Tarkington; 1858—Martha Tarkington Stewart; and 1879—Mary Stewart Carey and Martha Carey. Mary Stewart Carey was one of the founders of the Children's Museum of Indianapolis, the largest children's museum in the world.

The Tarkington family has figured in Indiana history for two centuries. Its most famous member was Booth Tarkington (1869–1946), a novelist and dramatist. Tarkington immortalized the wholesomeness of life in America's heartland in *Penrod, Penrod and Sam*, and the play *Seventeen*. He was awarded two Pulitzer Prizes for literature, one in 1919 for *The Magnificent Ambersons*, the other in 1922 for *Alice Adams*. The quiltmaker was Booth Tarkington's great-grandmother.

Wool Medallion Quilt

Wool Medallion. Pieced utility quilt. Maker unknown. Southwestern Indiana. Circa 1830.
Wool, wool batting, wool backing in fourteen pieces. 78½" × 69½". Collection of Peggy Taylor.

Checkers

Sheepfold or Nine-Patch. Family name is Checkers.
Unknown maker and location. Possibly Randolph County, Indiana. Circa 1830. Cotton. 87¾" × 79½".
Collection of Dr. and Mrs. Robert Blake.

Pink, blue, and white cotton prints alternate with plain blocks to form the center of this quilt, which is framed by a wide border of roller-printed fabrics.

This delicate beauty is quilted diagonally by hand with hand-spun thread at ten stitches to the inch.

Margaret Newby and Her Daughters

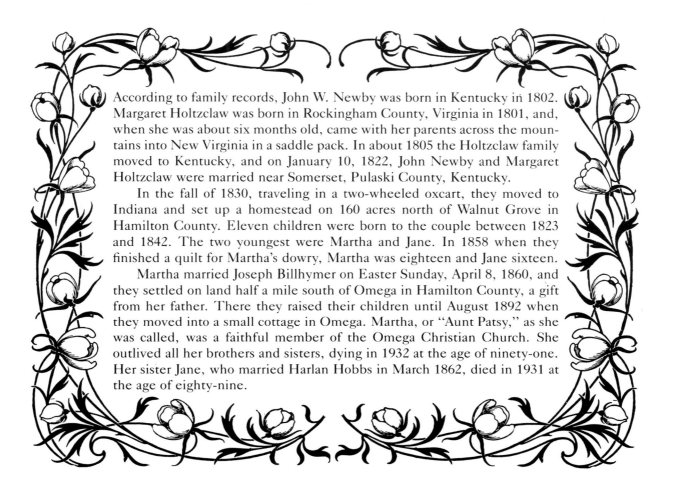

According to family records, John W. Newby was born in Kentucky in 1802. Margaret Holtzclaw was born in Rockingham County, Virginia in 1801, and, when she was about six months old, came with her parents across the mountains into New Virginia in a saddle pack. In about 1805 the Holtzclaw family moved to Kentucky, and on January 10, 1822, John Newby and Margaret Holtzclaw were married near Somerset, Pulaski County, Kentucky.

In the fall of 1830, traveling in a two-wheeled oxcart, they moved to Indiana and set up a homestead on 160 acres north of Walnut Grove in Hamilton County. Eleven children were born to the couple between 1823 and 1842. The two youngest were Martha and Jane. In 1858 when they finished a quilt for Martha's dowry, Martha was eighteen and Jane sixteen.

Martha married Joseph Billhymer on Easter Sunday, April 8, 1860, and they settled on land half a mile south of Omega in Hamilton County, a gift from her father. There they raised their children until August 1892 when they moved into a small cottage in Omega. Martha, or "Aunt Patsy," as she was called, was a faithful member of the Omega Christian Church. She outlived all her brothers and sisters, dying in 1932 at the age of ninety-one. Her sister Jane, who married Harlan Hobbs in March 1862, died in 1931 at the age of eighty-nine.

Margaret Holtzclaw Newby and her husband, John W. Newby.

The home-dyed red, blue, and green fabrics retain their deep rich colors in this quilt, which has remained unwashed after 160 years. The Tumbling Block composed of three diamonds was a popular all-over pattern and many combinations were possible. Here the white pieces form two different stars throughout the design. Hand-pieced and hand-quilted in the same all-over pattern with eight stitches to the inch, it has a thin cotton batting and quarter-inch binding.

Margaret Holtzclaw Newby (1801–1890) was the mother of the two young women, Martha and Jane, who made the appliqued quilt pictured below.

The Tea Box quilt was registered by Esther Applegate Foster, a great-great-granddaughter of the maker. An enthusiastic supporter of the Indiana Quilt Registry Project, Mrs. Foster registered family quilts from four generations before her death in January 1988.

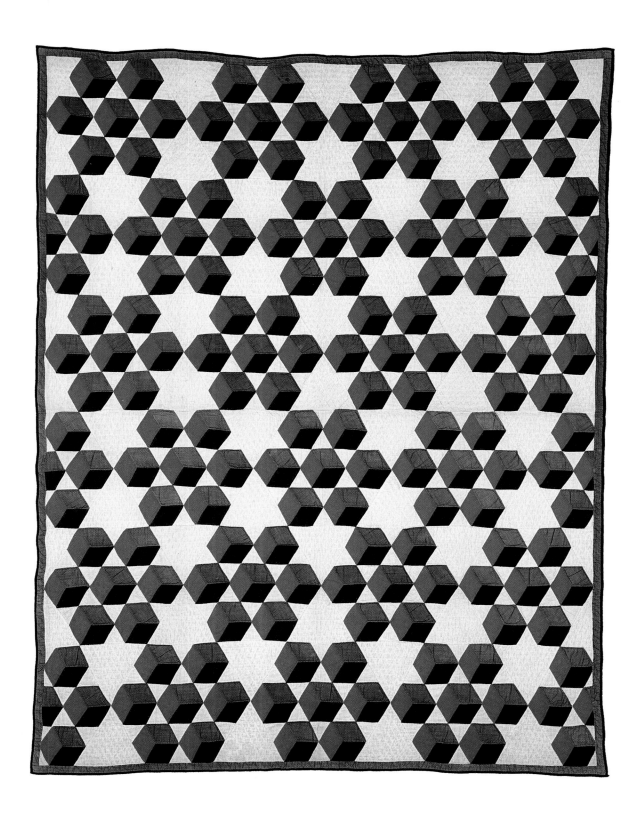

Margaret Newby's Tea Box

Tea Box. Pattern also called Tumbling Blocks. Pieced quilt made by Margaret Holtzclaw Newby.
Marion County, Indiana. 1830. Cotton. 84" × 64". Collection of Harry Foster.

Martha Newby Billhymer (1840–1932) is shown with five of her six children.
She outlived all but one, dying at the age of ninety-one.

Amaranth was one of the most unusual designs brought to the Indiana Quilt Registry. The amount of deterioration in the red fabric only slightly dims the character of this bold 30″ × 30″ block design. Only the side to the front of this appliqued quilt has a 7½″ border. Perhaps the bed was placed against the wall and only one border was required, or perhaps the young women were unsure about how to place the blocks.

The overall quilting in hanging diamonds and parallel lines measures an uneven eight stitches to the inch—the usual result of having more than one quilter. The green fabric is turning yellow in some areas owing to the use of fugitive dyes. The thin cot-

ton batting shows some seeds or debris when held to the light, and the quilt is edged with a thin, straight applied green binding.

When the Newby sisters embroidered their names, "Martha and Jane," onto the completed quilt in 1858, they could not have known what the future held in store. In 1987, during the first year of the Indiana Quilt Registry Project, Martha's great-grand-daughter—the present owner of the quilt—and Jane's great-granddaughter would discover each other because of this quilt and become friends. Second cousins, the women were living less than twenty miles apart, but were previously unknown to each other.

Amaranth

*Amaranth. Appliqued quilt. Made by sisters Martha Newby Billhymer and Jane Newby Hobbs.
White River Township, Hamilton County, Indiana. 1858. Cotton. 85" × 67".
Collection of Mary M. Clemans.*

Grandmother Brown's Peony

Appliqued quilt. Made by Margaret Bright Morgan Brown. Fredericksburg, Washington County, Indiana. Circa 1830. Cotton. 86¼" × 77". Collection of William Allen Reiner.

This is a very orderly, beautiful red and green quilt hand-appliqued on a natural background. Margaret Bright Morgan (1815–1902) was only sixteen when she made this formal, planned quilt. Young girls were expected to have a hope chest full of quilts by the time they married. Family history states that this one was made for that reason.

Miss Bright lived in Fredericksburg, Washington County, Indiana. According to family history, as a small child she presented flowers to the Marquis de Lafayette, the French hero of the American revolution, during his last visit to America in 1824, at Louisville, Kentucky.

Miss Bright married John Morgan and they were the parents of eight children. Her second marriage, to Alonzo B. Brown, resulted in one daughter, Annetta, who married Joseph Small in 1877 at Washington, Indiana. This couple's second daughter, Annetta Small, married Arthur Greenwood, who was an eight-term congressman from the old Second District in southern Indiana from 1923 to 1938.

Double T Quilt

Double T. Made by Margaret Williams. Location unknown, probably Pennsylvania. 1858.
Cotton. 94" × 78½". Collection of Tippecanoe County Historical Association.

A seven-inch applique border proudly proclaims the name of the quiltmaker, her birth date, and the year she made the quilt. The thirty traditional pieced Double-T blocks alternate with twenty plain blocks and are set on point.

The purple fabrics have faded to brown, indi-cating a dye change, but the quilting efforts of Margaret Williams (1822-?) will not be forgotten.

This quilt was donated in 1953 by a family member who referred to her Great-Aunt Peggy as a Quaker from Pennsylvania.

Mary Jane Kirkpatrick Harlan.

Jemima Harlan McIntosh (1862–1928), seated,
and her daughter, Ocie McIntosh Havens
(1888–1960), second and third generation
owners of the quilt.

Mary Jane Kirkpatrick was born in Rush County, Indiana, in 1832. Her father, David Kirkpatrick, had been born in Kentucky, and her mother, Jane Oldham, was from Tennessee. Jane had emigrated to Indiana at the age of five, riding horseback all the way, according to family legend.

In February 1852 Mary Jane married Samuel Harlan, a farmer and Baptist minister. They had six children, three boys and three girls. This magnificent quilt, a tribute to Mary Jane's needlework skills, has been passed down in the family: first to her own daughter, Jemima Jane Harlan McIntosh, then to Jemima's daughter, Ocie McIntosh Havens, then to Ocie's daughter, Betty Havens Vehslage, the current owner.

The quilt is a visual delight. The main designs are the urns with flowers that are appliqued lengthwise. The overall design is unified with the same green print and Turkey red fabrics. The embroidery, done with indigo-dyed two-ply cotton thread, provides exciting accents. The grapevine sprays found in profusion over the entire surface are embroidered in layers, are unstuffed, and form tiny grapes or berries. Birds perch on branches or stems, finished with embroidered details. A Turkey red leaf design appliqued onto the base of almost every green leaf provides even more continuity and pleasure in the visual effect. On one end, quilted sprays of rosebuds, not yet bursting into bloom, join the flowers coming from the border. The scalloped swag border, red and green on three sides, gives way to yellow and green on the fourth. The border shows a variation in the sawtooth application that merits additional study.

The quilting, eleven stitches to the inch, provides a double outline to most of the applique. Double diagonal parallel lines, less than an inch apart, cover the remaining surface of the quilt. Undoubtedly this was Mary Jane's "best quilt," made for her dowry.

Great-Grandmother's Quilt

Great-Grandmother's Quilt. Appliqued and embroidered quilt. Made by Mary Jane Kirkpatrick Harlan. Rush County, Indiana. Circa 1850. Cotton. 85" × 70". Collection of Betty Havens Vehslage.

Six Ramsay sisters, America Evaline (1832–1855), Ann Clarendia (1836–1859), Margaret Louisa (1838–1860), Armilda Jane (1840–1856), Sara Cacilda (1841–1918), and Mary Elizabeth (1844–1861), made this red, green, and yellow poinsettia applique. The applique work and quilting with eleven stitches to the inch are both of fine quality. The sisters left behind a number of quilts that were passed down through the family in a special trunk.

The twelve applique blocks are each eighteen inches square and the vining applique border shows leaves and holly. Double ball fringe in two colors was once attached to three sides of the quilt giving it an up/down orientation. The quilting motifs in the applique blocks are straight and diagonal lines and triple hanging diamonds, while in the borders feathers are used along with triple hanging diamonds.

William and Jane C. Burk Ramsay had eight children—seven daughters and one son. Most of the family died of tuberculosis at a young age; three of the sisters were in their early twenties and two were only sixteen. The family burial plot was at Pizgah Cemetery south of Rockville.

The present owner, Helen Farrow Risley, is the great-granddaughter of Sara Cacilda Ramsay Earp Farrow.

Ramsay Sisters Poinsettia

Poinsettia. Appliquéd quilt. Made by the six Ramsay sisters. Russellville, Putnam County, Indiana.
Circa 1850. Cotton. 92" × 77". Collection of Mrs. Hobart L. Risley.

Benjamin F. Biggs.

Detail of center of Biggs quilt.

Benjamin Franklin Biggs (1817–1883) and Elizabeth Gross were married January 11, 1849, about three months after this quilt was completed. In the spring of 1851, the newlyweds with some of their relatives journeyed in covered wagons from Maryland across the mountains, and after six weeks travel arrived in Lafayette, Indiana, where they made their home.

Benjamin was originally a millwright, but disliked the traveling that it entailed, so he took a position as foreman in a pump factory. He eventually bought the factory; the Biggs Pump Company continues to operate in Lafayette under different owners. He and Elizabeth were the parents of four children: two sons who died in childhood, and two daughters.

The inked signatures of friends and relatives remain easy to read in this 1848 beauty. It was made in the Millersburg, Maryland, area south of Baltimore, and is in the Baltimore Album style popular in the eastern United States during this period. Each sixteen-inch block is quilted with a different motif, with ten stitches to the inch. The border is quilted with tulips and hearts.

The quilt is predominantly red, green, and white; the center block has blue touches and four inked poems. The block next to the center reads "by the ladies for Benjamin Franklin Biggs 1848." The poems in the center block read as follows:

> Flowers seek the light, their beauties to display;
> The leaf will smile the same by night as day,
> Here is the smile that no cloud can overcast;
> The flowers and leaves are thine own to the last.
>
> The stars that gem life's morning sky,
> Smile sweetly over thee now;
> And flowers around thy pathway lie,
> And roses crown thy brow—.
>
> Should pleasure at its birth
> Fade like the hues of even[ing]
> Turn then away from earth,
> There's rest for thee in Heaven.
>
> Life is but a shadow—save a promise given
> Which lights up sorrow with a fadeless day.
> I touch the sceptre—with a hope in heaven;
> Come, turn thy spirit from the world away.

Benjamin Biggs's Quilt

Signature sampler. Appliqued quilt. Made "by the ladies for Benjamin Biggs." Millersburg, Frederick County, Maryland, 1848. Cotton, 100" × 100". Collection of the Tippecanoe County Historical Association.

Comforts in the Conflict: Civil War Era Quilts

2 "Indiana knows no East, no West, no North, no South, nothing but the Union." Governor Joseph A. Wright (served 1849–1857) had these ominous words inscribed on a block of stone taken from Saluda Landing, Jefferson County, as Indiana's contribution to a memorial to George Washington. They were indicative of the troubles to come.

Before the war, strong feelings against slavery existed in Indiana and many Hoosiers were actively engaged in the so-called Underground Railroad, an escape network to help escaped slaves travel north to Canada without being recaptured and returned to their southern masters. Several Underground Railroad routes ran through Indiana. The man called the president of the Underground Railroad was Levi Coffin, a Quaker businessman in Newport (now called Fountain City). Coffin and his helpers are credited with aiding in the escape of over 3,000 slaves.

When President Lincoln sounded the alarm after the attack on Fort Sumter, Oliver P. Morton, then serving as acting governor (he was elected in his own right in 1864), telegraphed Lincoln: "On behalf of the state of Indiana, I tender you for the defense of the nation, and to uphold the authority of the Government, ten thousand men." Within a week, 30,000 Indiana men had volunteered for the Union Army.

The only recorded battle of the Civil War to occur in Indiana was in 1863 when Confederate General John Hunt Morgan led a cavalry troop, nicknamed Morgan's Raiders, north out of Kentucky and crossed the Ohio River to Corydon before turning east into Ohio. Elsewhere, Indiana regiments participated bravely in major battles, from Bull Run through Vicksburg and Gettysburg to Appomattox. Indiana's death toll for the war totaled 25,000 men— only 7,000 in battle, the rest from disease.

Future Indiana governor Ira J. Chase was a schoolteacher in Barrington, Illinois, in 1859 when he met and married Rhoda Jane Castle. When the Civil War broke out, Chase was the first volunteer from his town to enlist. He fought in Missouri, Kentucky, and Tennessee in the first year of the war before he was confined to an army hospital at Nashville, Tennessee, with an illness.

His wife came to nurse him, bringing along their child. Army rules prevented her from taking care of him without first enlisting as an Army nurse. Rhoda promptly joined the Union Army as a nurse so that she could tend her husband. Following the war, Ira Chase joined the ministry, serving as pastor of the Christian Church at Mishawaka and later at LaPorte, Wabash, and Danville, Indiana. He served as governor from 1891 to 1893.

As a result of her heroism, the Indiana legislature in 1921 authorized a pension of $100 per month for Mrs. Chase, who had lost her eyesight from smallpox contracted while serving in the Civil War.

There was suffering and hardship for those at home, as well. With the men away many women were burdened not only with worry for their absent loved ones but also with responsibility for running farms and businesses. Women also worked as nurses and as volunteers, collecting money, books, food, and clothing for the Indiana soldiers. It was a long, grim conflict, and although the fighting ended in 1865, the scars would remain long into the twentieth century.

The sweeping changes that were taking place in the country by the mid-eighteenth century were reflected in the quilt world. The quadrant style quilt was dropped in favor of smaller blocks. A nine-block style was popular. Applique was still being done, but elaborate whitework was seen less and less. Whitework is a term used to refer to those white whole-cloth quilts that show evidence of stuffing or cording. Whitework did continue after the Civil War, but most of it was done by machine. Machine woven styles of white bedcovers were called Marseilles coverlets. They appear to be quilts because they have a top, filler, and backing, but the edges of the piece confirm that it was woven on a loom. Their nickname, Marseilles coverlets, is derived from the port of Marseilles, France, from which many examples were imported to this country.

Pieced quilts became more numerous. Log cabin styles developed and quilts using small pieces were popular. Small unit quilts included the Irish Chain, Trip around the World, Mosaic, and Boston Commons. The scrap quilt was coming of age. Numerous small pieces could be recycled in these styles.

Magazines such as *Godey's Lady's Book* and *The American Woman's Home* stressed the personal touch in home decorating. Fashionable mid-nineteenth century fabrics included silk, velvet, damask, plush, plain satin, and figured chintz. The latter was primarily used in bedchambers and for summer spreads. A new fabric for the period was a lightweight twilled wool challis printed in colorful floral designs, which often graced the back and border of quilts. All of these fabrics found their way into quilts of this and future generations.

Large Stars and Mariner's Compass, a multi-pointed star, continued to be made, as well as the appliqued Princess Feather or Prince's Feather pattern, first stitched in the early part of the nineteenth century following a trip to this country by the Prince of Wales.

The war brought grief to many women, who constructed "memory quilts" from the clothing of their departed loved ones or from the mourning attire worn by the survivors.

Mary Latta Merandy with her husband, John.

After President Lincoln's death in April 1865, the first of twelve funeral services would begin in the White House, and his body would be buried twenty days later in Springfield, Illinois, after a slow 1,700-mile journey by train. Lincoln had lived in Indiana from about eight years of age until he was twenty-one, and was considered an Indiana farm-boy.

The White House catafalque had an eleven-foot-high canopy made of black alpaca, draped with the finest black velvet, festooned with black crepe and enormous black satin rosettes. The special $1,500 coffin, made of walnut, was totally covered in the finest black broadcloth and padded with a white quilted satin lining.

When the funeral train reached Indianapolis on Sunday morning, April 30, 1865, the city was draped in black, and the columns of the State House were wrapped in barber-pole stripes of black crepe, in anticipation of the assassinated president lying in state within. Plans for a giant procession were cancelled due to torrents of rain that fell on the city, and viewing of the body was done on the funeral train.

William Robert Latta owned an Indianapolis restaurant at which Lincoln had dined several years before, and after the day's events Latta purchased some of the black fabric used to decorate the State House. His wife, Rebecca, and their daughter Mary used the black mourning crepe to make a Log Cabin quilt, adding red, green plaid, and pink fabric.

The forty-eight pieced blocks are constructed of folded strips placed in a Barn-Raising pattern, using the red center squares to signify the hearth of the log cabin, so important in Lincoln's early life in Indiana. The lining is unwashed maroon glazed cotton with double narrow black stripes, and the binding is an applied flat red braid. The original fabrics are faded now, but the treasured heirloom remains in very good condition.

The relationships among members of the Latta family are uncertain, but it is known that Mary, who helped make the quilt, and Alice, who later inherited it, were stepsisters. Perhaps Alice was William Latta's daughter and Mary was his wife's daughter from a previous marriage. In any case, Alice Latta Peele passed the quilt to her daughter, Ina Peele Schrock, who in turn passed it to her great-grand-nephew, the current owner.

The Lincoln Log Cabin

Log Cabin. Barn-Raising set. Pieced quilt.
Made by Alice Rebecca Driggs Latta and her daughter Mary Latta. Indianapolis, Marion County, Indiana.
1865–66. Cotton, wool, silk. 79" × 68". Collection of Gregg Townsend.

James and Melanie Schmidt Schultheiss.

This striking patriotic quilt was an original design pieced by Melanie Schmidt Schultheiss (1842–1933) for her husband, James Jacob, in 1902, to commemorate his Civil War service. It is inscribed:

> The flag that my dear husband James
> Schultheiss fought under three years five
> months 21 days from 1861–1865
> Made by your wife Melanie S in 1902

The quilt contains forty-two pieced blocks and thirty plain blocks and is surrounded by red and white borders with blue binding.

Her marriage to James was the sequel to a tragic love story. Melanie's boy friend had gone to fight in the Civil War while she stayed in Indianapolis and worked in the kitchen of her father's saloon at the northwest corner of Delaware and South Streets. One day a young soldier came to the saloon and asked for Melanie, introducing himself as James Schultheiss. He had been a trench mate of her boy friend and had talked with him about his home, friends, and Melanie. He made him a promise to deliver any bad news in person to Melanie. James told Melanie of his buddy's death and offered his sympathy, then asked if he could call on her again. She agreed and they courted, fell in love, and were married on July 2, 1865.

Melanie was a native of Strasbourg, Alsace (now part of France), who had immigrated to the United States before the Civil War. James (1843–1928) had been born at Haubstadt in Gibson County. In 1861 he joined Company G, 60th Infantry of the Union Army. He fought in the battles of Shiloh, Corinth, Stone River, Arkansas Post, Vicksburg, and Appomattox. Several times he entered the enemy's lines as a spy, and was successful in obtaining the information sought and escaping back into his own lines. He was taken prisoner half a dozen times, but always managed to make his escape, according to *Jennings County Biographical Souvenir Sketches*, 1889. James was a charter member of the Seymour Post of the GAR and also of the Indianapolis Post.

James and Melanie became the parents of twelve children and settled in Seymour, Indiana, where they attended St. Ambrose Catholic Church. James was a carpenter by trade. The couple celebrated their sixty-second wedding anniversary before he died in 1928. Melanie died in 1933, age ninety.

Flags for James and Melanie

Flag quilt. Pieced. Made by Melanie Schmidt Schultheiss. Seymour, Jackson County, Indiana. 1902.
Cotton. 78" × 68". Collection of Kay Denning.

Julia Ann Garrett Swearingen (1876–1960) was a young married woman in 1901 when she made the Ku Klux Klan quilt from her father's KKK robe.

John Garrett (1845–1929), a Union Army soldier wounded during Sherman's attack on Atlanta, joined the original Ku Klux Klan soon afterwards.

John Garrett was a Yankee from Indiana who served with the Union Army in the Civil War. He was severely wounded during Sherman's attack on Atlanta, and carried the pain of his wounds the rest of his life. For reasons of his own, John joined the Ku Klux Klan, defined by *Webster's Dictionary* as "a secret society founded about 1865 to oppose the granting of privileges to freed Negroes." The robes for members of the original Klan were homemade from makeshift patterns in a variety of fabrics and colors. While family history does not confirm the color or colors of John Garrett's robe, family descendents presume it was red. The original KKK was suppressed in the 1870s, but there continued to be many vigilante or night-rider groups, especially in the south. When the Klan was reactivated in the early 1920s as a "Protestant organization for white supremacy," the robes were standardized—all white and factory-made.

Julia Ann Garrett, John's daughter, was born in 1876 in Peru, Indiana, and was married on her twen-tieth birthday, February 21, 1896, to Lonzo Erdon Swearingen. In 1901 her younger sister, Elsie Garrett, and her mother, Elizabeth Roquet Garrett, helped Julia Ann make the quilt, cutting the Ku Klux Klan robe into pieces but preserving it as a family heirloom. Julia Ann was to die on her eighty-fourth birthday in 1960. The current owner is her grandson, the great-grandson of John Garrett.

This quilt is twenty-four one-template pieced red and white blocks that alternate in simplicity with twenty-four white blocks. The slashes of red issue a statement. Nearly half the blocks have been constructed in opposite directions, but the setting with white blocks and white border brings unity to the overall design. The quilt was machine-pieced but hand-quilted, in an uneven seven stitches to the inch. The front and back have been turned under and stitched. There is no other binding. One name for the quilt, Old Crow, brings instant recognition and wonder at the choice of pattern.

The Ku Klux Klan Quilt

Ku Klux Klan quilt. Pattern also called Windmill or Old Crow.
Pieced quilt made by Julia Ann Garrett Swearingen. Peru, Miami County, Indiana. 1901. Cotton.

This photograph of Susan and Green McCord, taken about 1885, is the only existing photographic portrait of the couple and is reproduced here through the courtesy of the Henry Ford Museum.

Susan McCord's Harrison Rose quilt is a splendid example of mid nineteenth century applique. Named for William Henry Harrison, first governor of the Indiana Territory and ninth president of the United States, the Harrison Rose pattern was very popular in the Midwest from 1840 to 1880. The quilt is made primarily of Turkey red and green fabric on a natural background. Touches of pink are added in the smaller blossoms.

The highly stylized urns are decorated with antimony orange insets. The Harrison Roses which dominate the urn design are identified by the triangular shapes that circle the outside edges of the roses. Decorative blanket and chain stitch embroidery was used with the flowers in place of fabric for stems.

The wide appliqued borders are of flowers and vines, but each border features a different flower—a signature among Susan McCord quilts. All of her appliques are done with a whip stitch instead of a hidden stitch. The leaves in the urns show a similarity to another popular pattern of the time, the Princess Feather. The two long-stemmed flowers flanking the centered Harrison rose, often called Mexican Roses, became popular following the Mexican War in 1848.

The binding features piping and cording which are quite sophisticated for a quilt made in a rural area. The batt is very thin, and cotton debris can be viewed from the back of the quilt. This was probably a summer spread or Sunday best bedcover.

Susannah (Susan) Noakes was born in Decatur County, Indiana, on October 7, 1829. She married Green McCord in 1849 and they settled in McCordsville, Indiana, a town named for his ancestors. A farm wife with seven children, Susan had an interest in gardening and homeopathic medicines that were derived from herbs, roots, bark, leaves, and vegetables. She died at the age of eighty on December 12, 1909, from complications following an accident on her farm. A cow kicked her while she was milking, and she suffered a broken hip and exposure from the cold December weather. Pneumonia and peritonitis were the cause of death.

In addition to this quilt, Susan McCord made other appliques, pieced quilts, pieced block repeats with appliqued borders, and crazy quilts. The Henry Ford Museum in Dearborn, Michigan, purchased a total of ten Susan McCord quilts from her family in 1973.

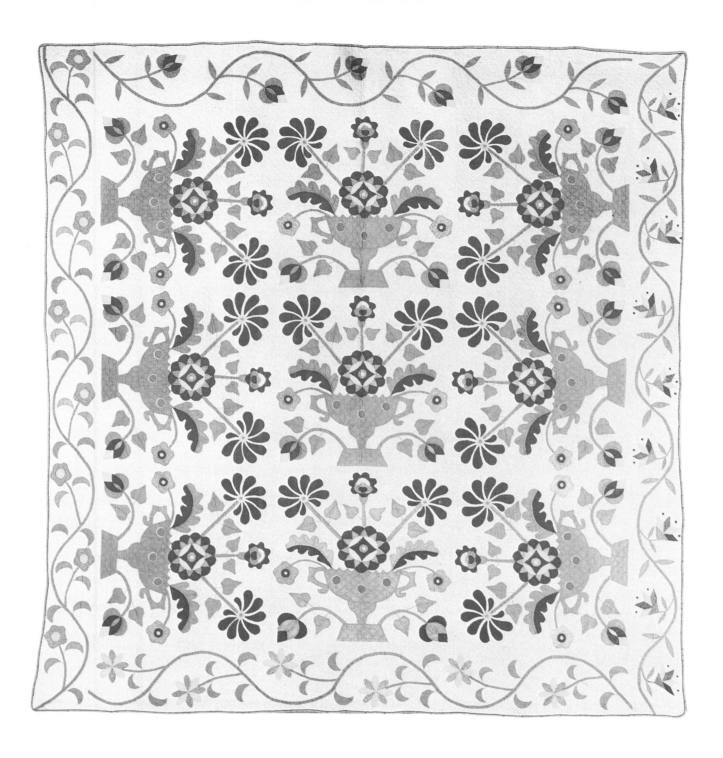

The Harrison Rose Quilt

Harrison Roses in Urns. Appliqued quilt. Made by Susan Noakes McCord. McCordsville, Hancock County, Indiana. Circa 1860. Cotton. 81" × 76½". Collection of the Henry Ford Museum.

Susan Brackney Clayton (1848–1942) made the Mariner's Compass quilt. In this photograph, taken a year before she died, the eighty-two-year-old quilt hangs behind her.

Susan Brackney was born in 1848 in Brazil, Clay County, Indiana, to Marmduke and Nancy Moore Brackney. Her father was an Ohioan who in 1836 purchased 80 acres of Indiana land. In 1858, when she was only ten, Susan began the Mariner's Compass for her dowry; with some help from her family, the quilt was finished by the time she was twelve.

In 1871 Susan married Dave Clayton, and they took the quilt with them when they went to live in Kansas for one year, 1872–1873. After they returned to the Midwest, they lived for a time in Minnesota and Illinois, but in 1888 they went to homestead in Nebraska. Again they traveled by covered wagon, and again the quilt went with them. During their four years in the sod house on the prairie near Elton, Custer County, Nebraska, Susan wrote hauntingly of her memories and homesickness for her family in Indiana.

Not yet forty years old and separated from her family and those dear to her, Susan Brackney Clayton wrote the following from her home in Arthur, Illinois, on June 18, 1886. Her writings provide the excuse for the care, protection, and preservation of the beloved Mariner's Compass, to make that tangible link with her childhood and her family last her whole life through, to make it available to her sight and touch, to soothe the heart within.

It is difficult to imagine a child of ten undertaking such an ambitious project. The pattern is certainly not a simple one, nor is this a scrap quilt. The thin dark blue star, the pink star with the matching center, and the large brown background points match in every block. Only the outside points are made of scraps.

True, it lacks perfect symmetry: there is no sashing on one side. However, when made for use on a bed against the wall, any type of border there would have been unnecessary. The fabrics probably came from the family's own Olds & Brackney General Store, which Susan's father owned with another relative. The dark fabrics show some color changes owing to the fugitive dyes used at the time, and the backing is coarsely woven and uses three strips, 31″, 31″, and 10″ in width. A ⅜″ straight applied binding finishes the edges, and brown and natural colored threads were used in the quilting.

THE BOOK OF MEMORY*

As I open the book of memory and scan life pages through
What joys what pleasures and sorrow and pain [are] written
   therein

There is no book we can remember so well as the book
   of memory
As we turn the leaves and read the pages through we
   see many
happy faces smile on us who have long since crossed the
   unknown
sea and many more who are scattered here and there.

As we read of the many places where we have been we
   see the
grandure of earth and all of the beautiful scenery which God
has made . . . as we scan the pages through we read of
   the old
home and our childhood days

What pleasure, what happiness, what sorrow and pain
Oh memory, it is God's best gift of all
Without the great gift of memory our lives would be like
an unwritten book and all would be blank . . .

* portions of the original with corrections

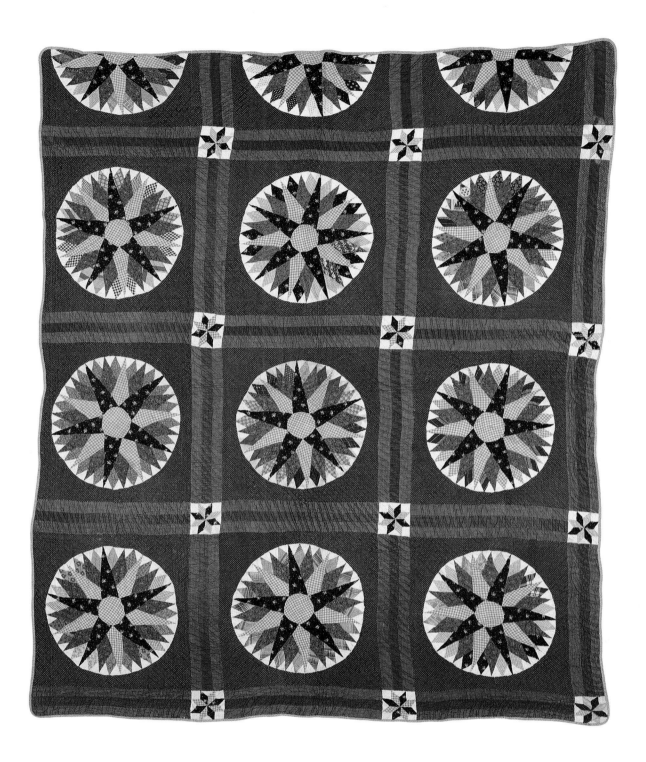

Susan Brackney's Mariner's Compass

Mariner's Compass. Pattern also called Chips and Whetstones. Pieced quilt.
Made by Susan Brackney Clayton. Brazil, Clay County, Indiana. 1858–1860. Cotton. 87½″ × 74″.
Collection of Mary Kompst Taylor.

Susan Brackney Clayton.

MEMORIES OF THE OLD HOME PLACE

Note: While homesteading in Nebraska with her husband in 1890, far from her home and family, Susan Brackney Clayton wrote the following. It is evident she poignantly remembered a life in faraway Indiana that was simply not available to her in that sod house on the prairie. The spelling is left as written. Where absolutely necessary, a bracketed correction has been inserted following the word.

How my thoughts wonder far away to Indiana where I spent my childhood days on the old home place

How well I remember every hill and hollow and every nook and corner and the great yellow willows that over hung the branches on the old home place

How us children used to roump over those old fields and pastures and gather the great red berrys and the golden buttercups and the violets on the old home place

There was the old burch [birch] creek where brother Duke and I caught many a long string of [fish] We loved that old burch creek by the old home place

How us children used to climb the apple trees and gather great red and golden apples There was four great orchards on the old home place

There was the old barn too with its four great rooms and to [two] great sheds how us children ust to romp and play hide and seak in that old barn on the old home place

Brother Duke and I ust to ride the horses round and round to tramp the wheat out that was spread on the old barn floor on the old home place

And the neighbors would come from far and near and bring their wheat to tramp it out upon that great barn floor on the old home place

Yes there was the grave yard to up in the sugar camp where brother Joe and Sister Abbie and little sisters Liddie and Losie and wee little brother too was burried on the old home place

There was our new little school house just a little peace down the lain How us children ust to romp and play at noon on the old home place

But the years went gleaming on down the eternal grove of time and our child hood days were fast and we were no longer children on the old home place

And we are catered [scattered] now and gone to make homes of our own and never again will we gather around that old fire place on the old home place

By Susan Brackney Clayton
April 4, 1890
Elton, Nebraska

Forget-me-not. Homesteading in Nebraska, Susan Clayton penned this
plea to a beloved sister back home in Indiana.

The picture of the ninety-three-year-old Susan Brackney Clayton with her quilt is a most unusual piece of documentation that will always be passed down with the quilt, from generation to generation, to daughters or nieces in the family. Now 130 years old, the quilt is nearly as bright as when Susan cut the pieces as a child. It is in excellent condition, a tribute to the value and sentiment placed upon it by this woman and her descendents. Susan died in Cisna, Illinois, in her ninety-fourth year, after keeping the quilt in her own possession an incredible eighty-two years! Her grandniece, the quilt's current owner, was well acquainted with her Aunt Sue and still marvels at her remarkable memory:

She had total recall, and stories of her experiences not only recalled the exact dates but the time of day and the weather at the time. We loved to ask her to tell us stories, and after a while she would ask us to read to her for a bit. After a time Aunt Sue would take over and recite the Bible from memory.

Her parents eventually had eighteen children, though several died very young. While her brothers were needed to work in the family sawmill, her father wanted the girls to have an education, and he felt Aunt Sue was the brightest and therefore the one to receive the most education.

This grandniece who has inherited the treasured Mariner's Compass declares, "It will stay in the family. It is already willed to the next owner."

Susan Brackney Clayton's diary entry,
Elton, Nebraska, July 15, 1890:

. . . far away on western prairie wild
I can look as far as my eyes will let me see . . .
far away in the distance I can see the green hills almost
reaching the deep blue skyes and in places the
clouds seam to be kissing the hills and
wetting their cheeks with there tears . . .
it is one vast prairie there is not a tree
nothing but hills and carrions to mar the seen
but the wind is always whisling round the house
with one bitter moan and seems
like the voice of the dead calling to me . . .
how lonely it seems away out here away from
all the noise and clammer of citty life
where all is piece and quiat nothing to mar the
   stillness except
the whispering wind it seems
only to be a moaning refrain.

Sarah Cortwright Elston.

Sarah Cortwright (1841–1931) was only sixteen when she made this quilt in 1857. The seventy-eight scrap nine-patch diamonds alternate with sixty navy blue dot diamond blocks. The result is modern looking even though the quilt was made over 130 years ago.

Sarah married Lewis Elston on Halloween, 1863. They had a dairy farm near Westtown, New York, where Lewis also did carpentry and built wagons.

The diamond shape that Sarah used was more frequently seen as six-pointed stars. The quilt has been passed through the family and is presently owned by the great-great-granddaughter-in-law.

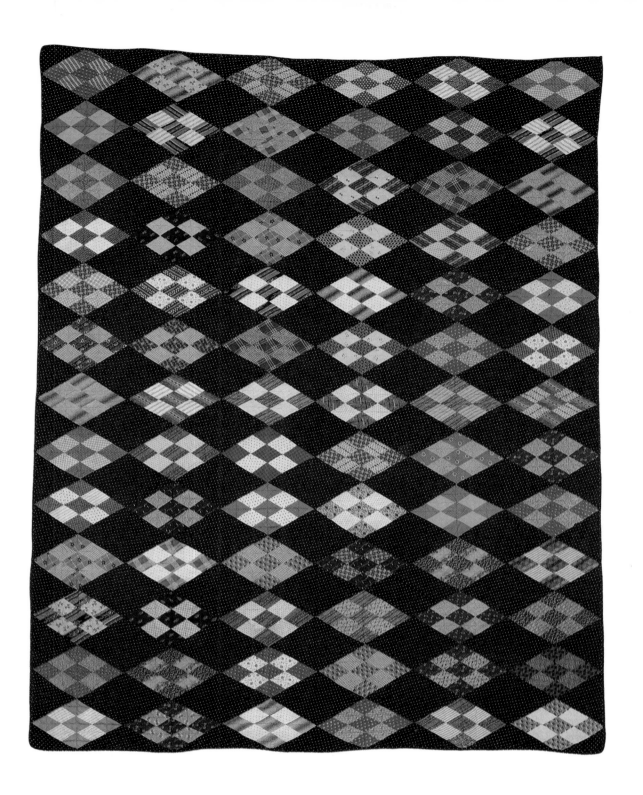

Sarah's Nine-Patch Diamond

Nine-patch Diamond. Pieced quilt. Made by Sarah Cortright Elston. Greenville, New York. 1857. Cotton. 89" × 71". Collection of Jeri Booth.

Mrs. Havekotte's Rose Quilt

Harrison Rose variation. Appliqued quilt. Made by Sophiah Holle Havekotte.
Huntersville, Franklin County, Indiana. 1860. Cotton. 92" × 88". Collection of Alberta J. Staley.

One of the most intriguing quilts found in the registry was this appliqued Harrison Rose variation. It is dated 1860 in the upper left corner and initialed "HH" in the lower left corner, and in the lower right corner the maker appliqued her first name, Sophiah, in her own handwriting—an unusual technique for the time. The initials "HH" could stand for Holle and Havekotte, Sophiah's maiden and married names, or they could be her husband's initials; his name was Henry Nicholas Havekotte, and he was a

sheriff in Franklin County. (The Holle family farm was across the road from the Havekottes, so Sophiah married the boy next door.)

The quilt is done in red, green, and yellow applique on a white background. The colors and nine-block set confirm the 1860 date. Quilting outlines the appliqued shapes on the borders and blocks. Unfortunately, Sophiah didn't enjoy many years of quilting. Born in 1840, she died in 1865 when her youngest child, Matilda, was only seven years old.

44

Kate Pickle's Feathered Star

Feathered Star with Tulips. Pieced and appliqued quilt. Made by Kate Pickle. Knox County, Indiana.
Circa 1860. Cotton. 78½" × 68". Collection of Robert and Marjorie Myers.

A Feathered Star quilt is nearly always spectacular, but the addition of the red tulips makes this one truly extravagant. The tulip appliques in the stars' centers are given an extra flair with a thin green curve appliqued beneath the blooms. The exquisite quilting, at nine stitches to the inch, outlines the pieced and appliqued designs and forms feathered wreaths in the white areas and feathers in the borders.

The rich pink and orange blossoms in full bloom in the borders tend to soften the bright red of the tulips. The border seems an "afterthought" because the flowers are definitely a contrast to the tulips with

their pointed leaves and narrow, precise stems. The border is broken in opposite corners "to make it fit," while the Feathered Star blocks are quite exact. Regardless of the maker's original intentions, the quilt is close to perfection.

"Aunt" Kate Pickle made the Feathered Star for her adopted son, Joe Dutton. Kate was of German ancestry, lived in Knox County, and attended Presbyterian services at the Royal Oak Church, according to the family. The quilt has remained in the family, and now belongs to the great-grandson of the maker.

Julia Garvin was still in her teens when she created this legacy that is still magnificent after nearly 150 years. As with an optical illusion, the eye can't decide whether to watch the green feathered stars or the red rosettes between them. The points of the stars are lost in the seam allowances of the blocks, which have been set on point, yet it doesn't seem a flaw in this design but rather a complement.

Each rosette has a different design embroidered in its center. The smallest rosettes are centered in every half-block to form the first of the borders; the second border framing the quilt is composed of small red and white triangles, the same as those used to frame the stars. The third border, ten inches wide, has undulating vines encircling the quilt. Sprays of currants rotate among the fancy leaves, some of them red indicating ripeness, others antimony orange to show ripeness yet to come. Each of the four corner blocks of the border has a different floral wreath and still more of the small red and white triangles.

Quilting in double-line cross hatching fills the centers of the green stars and the outer border. The rosettes are surrounded with feathers and all the quilting is twelve stitches to the inch. There are some dye changes in the green fabric where tinges of blue are found, but the reds, pinks, and orange remain strong and true.

Perhaps this Feathered Star was the star of Julia's hope chest when she married Adam Yeakel on September 11, 1856. A gift to the museum by the family of her grandson, Carl Smith, the quilt is often displayed to the delight of visitors.

Julia's Feathered Star with Rosettes

Feathered Star with Rosettes. Pieced and appliqued quilt. Made by Julia Garvin Yeakel (1829–1918).
Prairie Township, Kosciusko County, Indiana. Circa 1845. Cotton. 81" × 80".
Collection of the Kosciusko County Jail Museum.

Amanda "Mandy" Harris, left, and Mary Jane Harris, right, made the colorful Star of Bethlehem quilt. It is interesting to note that the dresses of the sisters appear to be made of the same calico print.

Sisters Mandy (1832–1910) and Mary Jane Harris (1834–1910), both Putnam County housewives, made their star quilt as a gift for Henry Harris Underwood, their favorite nephew, about 1875. This dramatic star has masculine appeal with dark green and natural diamonds contrasted with pink and maroon. As further evidence of their fine needlework, Mandy and Mary Jane finished the edge of the quilt with a handsome red piping seldom seen on quilts.

Indiana Stars

Star of Bethlehem. Pieced quilt. Made by Amanda and Mary Jane Harris. Putnam County, Indiana.
Circa 1875. Cotton. 96½" × 90". Collection of Mrs. Ernest Reklis.

Lone Star by the Five Booher Sisters

Lone Star. Pieced quilt. Made by Adelaide Malera Booher Cragun. Whitestown, Boone County, Indiana. Circa 1880. Cotton, wool, and silk. 88¼" × 74½". Collection of the Boone County Historical Society.

In the days when large families were the rule rather than the exception, every member had to contribute his share. Adelaide Malera Booher (1857–1932) was from one such family in Boone County. She grew up with eleven brothers and sisters. Quilt making was probably a necessity to provide bed coverings for this large family.

When Addie, as she was called by her family, made her Lone Star quilt in the 1880s, four of her sisters—Emma, Margaret, Martha, and Minnie—helped her. More than the work was probably shared over the quilt frame while stitching this handsome star.

The star is in warm earth colors and has an unusual two-inch strip outlining it. It was a true scrap quilt, made from old clothing of cotton, wool, and silk.

Another Booher sisters quilt is in chapter 3.

Anna Clemmons's Star of Bethlehem

Star of Bethlehem. Pieced and appliqued quilt. Made by Anna Marie Arnold Clemmons. Probably Parke County, Indiana. Circa 1880. Cotton. 79¾" × 75". Collection of Mr. and Mrs. Richard Clemons.

Quilts have always been popular gifts; many are made to celebrate special occasions and events. Anna Clemmons (1842–1927) made a stunning Star of Bethlehem for her husband, Joseph Clemmons, in 1880 to commemorate his thirty-fourth birthday.

The embroidered inscription on the left corner of the quilt tells us that J. Clemmons married Anna M. Arnold in 1866 and the right corner message states that this quilt was "presented to J. Clemmons on his 34th birthday by his wife." The applique border is unusual on large star quilts; however, this one with its graceful swag offers the perfect frame for the bright star.

The current owners are related to the maker and her husband. Anna Clemmons's son, who was Richard Clemons's grandfather, fought bitterly with his brother and to break family ties changed the spelling of his last name by deleting an "m."

Elizabeth Innis Askren, who learned tailoring as a young woman, in later years made several masterpiece quilts, including the Pennsylvania Rose.

Elizabeth Innis Askren (1822–1893) emigrated from Ohio as a child to Milroy in Rush County, Indiana. She married James Campbell Askren (1827–1880) there at the Reformed Presbyterian Church. They had met when he was transporting a load of wheat from Ohio to New Albany. James built Elizabeth a three-story red brick house north of Milroy about 1860. According to family legend, the womenfolk used their bread pans to bake bricks for the house. The house has fourteen rooms and eleven fireplaces. The floors are of ash and walnut.

One of Elizabeth's masterpieces, an all-white whole-cloth quilt, won a prize of six coin silver teaspoons at one of the first Indiana State Fairs to have women's exhibits, in 1878. James Askren had carried the quilt on horseback to the fairgrounds at 19th and Alabama Streets in Indianapolis.

Elizabeth was proficient in tailoring and took to quilting easily, but it was her friend Jane Stewart who reportedly designed this Pennsylvania Rose quilt. It is made of red, green, pink, and yellow fabrics in small prints and solid colors on a background of white. Four blocks, each 24″ square, make up the quadrant-style center, which is framed by 13″-wide borders. Outline quilting surrounds the appliqued flowers, buds, and leaves. The background is quilted in crosshatch motif with fine even stitches.

Elizabeth died in 1893, but her quilts continue to win prizes at the Indiana State Fair competitions in the antique quilt category. One won as recently as 1984.

Elizabeth's Pennsylvania Rose Quilt

*Pennsylvania Rose. Appliqued quilt. Made by Elizabeth Innis Askren. Milroy, Rush County, Indiana. 1878.
Cotton. 86" × 79". Collection of Mildred Niesse.*

The Crazy Victorians

3 What we have chosen to call the Victorian era was a period of sweeping change in Indiana lifestyles. It saw the development of the urban environment, improvements in transportation, and rapid growth of manufacturing. Fewer goods were being made by families at home, more in factories—small family-owned establishments at first, but increasingly larger and more sophisticated ones later. In central Indiana in the 1880s natural gas was discovered, as a result of which such cities as Muncie, Anderson, and Kokomo became boom towns. The railroad revolutionized transportation, both for people and for agricultural and industrial products. At this time more people were living in towns or cities than ever before, and both men and women were taking a greater interest in politics.

The Victorian woman was the first to live in an age of technology. Electricity, telephones, sewing machines, indoor plumbing, and city water and sewage were some of the amenities available. Natural gas, coal, or steam heated her home and fueled her kitchen. She crowded her house with dark furniture, screens, and ornate draperies, and covered every surface with bric-a-brac, photographs, fans, and other adornments. In her new-found leisure time she painted china, did needlepoint and embroidery, and, like her female ancestors before her, continued to stitch on quilts. But they were quilts with a difference.

The quilts of the Victorian Age are distinctive. The most easily recognizable style from that era is the crazy quilt, so named because of the random way in which it was assembled to resemble pieces of a puzzle.

Crazy quilts were generally of two types: all-over and contained. The all-over type has a single piece of foundation that was used for all the pieces that were assembled. In the contained crazy, a piece of fabric destined to become a block, strip, or diamond in the top was used as a foundation upon which the patches and embroidery could be applied. The patched pieces were then sewn into the desired configuration and a backing covered all the stitching. This technique is sometimes called the pressed method. Crazy quilts were tacked in some manner, usually without a filler.

The crazy quilt was constructed using a foundation to which pieces of wool, silk, brocade, etc., were sewn. The seams were often embellished with embroidery stitches, and embroidery might be applied to the individual quilt patches as well. Since they had no filler, these crazy quilts were not meant to keep anyone warm on a cold night. Instead they graced the library table, piano, or fainting couch, serving as an expression of the artistic abilities of the woman of the house. Making a crazy quilt therefore could not have been a typical pastime in Indiana in earlier years, when leisure was virtually unknown to most women.

Another quilt type popular in the Victorian Age was the signature quilt. Whether used as a remembrance gift or a fund-raiser, the signature quilt is easily recognizable too. Names are written on the blocks with India ink or embroidered. Placement of the name might depend on the size of the donation to the project. The quilt might be quilted in the traditional manner, or tacked, depending upon the fabrics used. When finished, it might be auctioned or raffled to raise additional funds for the group.

Temperance quilts were another product of the Victorian Age. The Woman's Christian Temperance Union used the colors medium blue and white in their campaigns. A Drunkard's Path pattern assembled in these colors usually denotes a temperance quilt.

The scrap quilt is unique to American quilt history. Before the Industrial Revolution, every scrap of fabric was saved to patch and repatch bed coverings. This thriftiness became part of every household; even after fabrics became affordable and plentiful, many quilters continued to make their quilts from scraps left over from other home sewing projects.

The ultimate scrap quilt is a charm quilt, the popularity of which seems to run in cycles. Charm quilts were a fad during the Victorian era and again in the 1920s. There was increased interest in the charm quilt once again in the 1980s, with groups formed to share fabric and keep their quilts from be-coming prohibitively expensive. Charm quilts were often also called beggar quilts because the maker would beg or trade scraps with her family, friends, and neighbors. To make a charm quilt, the quilter collected fabrics, trading with others until she had no two pieces identical, and then proceeded to make the quilt in a single template design.

Charm quilts can reveal a great deal about a quilter's life, as the individual pieces of fabric tell stories of their own. One family had a tradition of placing the family charm quilt on the bed when one of the children was ill. It was a game for the sick child to try to locate "pairs" on the quilt. The family told us they called it their "measles and mumps quilt."

Male political figures in Oriental kimonos are hidden in each of the nine blocks of this masterpiece crazy quilt. The men seem to appear and disappear depending on the vantage point of the viewer. All the heads on the Oriental figures are believed to be such political figures as Thomas Hendricks, Claude Matthews, Daniel Vorhees, Eugene V. Debs, John Logan, and James G. Blaine. One political ribbon, the forerunner of the campaign button, reads "Cleveland-Hendricks Victory" and refers to the 1884 presidential campaign.

Hoosier Thomas Hendricks was elected governor in 1868 and 1872 and was an unsuccessful candidate for vice-president in the most disputed election in U.S. history, the Hayes-Tilden contest. Following this loss Hendricks returned to private legal practice until Grover Cleveland selected him as a running mate in 1884. Cleveland and Hendricks were victorious, but Hendricks died in Indianapolis in 1885, the fifth vice-president to die in office.

During the Civil War, when Morgan's Raiders rode through Kentucky, Indiana, and Ohio, Claude Matthews was a boy of sixteen. His father, fearful of losing his livestock to marauding soldiers, sent the lad to drive 500 mules to safety in Ross County, Ohio. On the trip, Claude met Martha Whitcomb, daughter of James Whitcomb, who had served as governor of Indiana from 1843 to 1848, during the time of the Mexican War. Claude and Martha married in 1868, and settled in Vermillion County, Indiana. Matthews was elected governor in 1892.

Labor leader Eugene V. Debs was born in Terre Haute in 1855. His role in the 1894 Pullman strike led to a six-month jail sentence and a national reputation. An idealistic crusader for social justice, he ran for president five times on the Socialist party ticket. Although widely respected in the state, he never won as much as six percent of the Indiana vote.

Blaine and Logan were the unsuccessful Republican candidates for president and vice-president in 1884. Vorhees was U.S. Senator from Indiana, 1860–72.

A variety of embellishments, from painted flowers and birds to political ribbons and scarves, have been used as decoration on this contained crazy quilt. The nine blocks are held together with impressive feather stitching, single, double, and triple. The back of the quilt is black and white checkered satin trimmed with red stitching.

The Indiana Political Crazy Quilt

Crazy quilt. Pressed method. Maker unknown. Terre Haute, Vigo County, Indiana. Circa 1890.
Velvet and satin. 64" × 60¼". Collection of the Vigo County Historical Society.

Harriet Haskell Adams (1838–1916), shown with her
daughter, Laura Adams (1874–1970), is the
maker of the Pineapple quilt.

This Pineapple variation of the Log Cabin pattern is constructed in vibrant colors—orange, brown, tan, gold, navy, and maroon. This quilt might be just another Pineapple except for the way the light strikes the design, spotlighting some areas and playing down others. A beautiful challis has been used for the backing.

Harriet Haskell was born in Chinango County, New York. At the age of ten, in 1848, she traveled west by canal boat and covered wagon to Illinois, then to Wisconsin. She married George Adams in Oshkosh on November 12, 1860. They had four children, one boy and three girls. The quilt's owner is a great-granddaughter of Harriet.

Pineapple Log Cabin

Pineapple Log Cabin. Pieced quilt. Pressed method. Harriet Haskell Adams.
Oshkosh, Winnebago County, Wisconsin. 1875–1876.
Velvet and silk. 67" × 65". Collection of Janet Burton.

Henrietta Weimer Rice (1849–1931) was artistically inclined. In addition to doing fancy needlework, she took art classes in Indianapolis and painted in oils on canvas and on velvet.

This elaborate crazy consists of thirty contained blocks of elegant fabrics: velvets, satins, silks, and chintz. There are many embellishments, and the intricate embroidery on the border displays outstanding workmanship. On the reverse side, a striking embroidered floral wreath medallion has been placed on a bright red silk background with embroidered and painted borders running the length of the quilt.

Henrietta Weimer Rice (1849–1931), who had received formal art training, was the wife of Charles Rice, president of the Camden State Bank. They had no children, and this quilt passed to her sister's family and her descendants. Henrietta finished her masterpiece with cording on the edges and double tassels with beading on all the corners.

Many crazy quilts have similar birds and flowers, because they were available in panels, patterns, and pictures in periodicals of the day.

Henrietta's Fancy Crazy Quilt

*Crazy quilt. Pieced quilt. Pressed method. Made by Henrietta Weimer Rice.
Camden, Carroll County, Indiana. Circa 1880.
Velvet, satin, silk, and chintz. 81" × 69". Collection of Betty Mayne.*

The Tumbling Blocks, Baby Blocks, or Tea Box pattern is an optical illusion created by the use of diamonds in light, medium, and dark color tones. Usually made of delicate fabrics, these quilts were made for show, to be used as parlor throws, much like crazy quilts.

Mary Henry's parents, Johanna Illender and John Henry, both came from England, met in Ohio, were married, and moved to Switzerland County, Indiana, about 1840. Quilt owner Charlotte Hudelson relates that "pieces of my great-grandmother's wedding dress are in that quilt." The dress was of gold damask and must have been very beautiful. John Henry built the Henry Ink Factory located one and a half miles west of Vevay, Indiana, in 1858. Here he also carried on his business as a printer and bookbinder. The ink manufactured at the factory was shipped to newspapers in Cincinnati, Louisville, St. Louis, and Pittsburgh.

Their four children were educated at home until Julia Dumont founded a school for boys and girls in Switzerland County, which John Henry allowed them to attend. In religion Mr. Henry was a Swedenborgian, and periodically traveled to Cincinnati to attend the nearest Church of the New Jerusalem with fellow Swedenborgian Ulysses P. Schenk. According to the *Abbingdon Dictionary of Living Religions*, the two churches of this denomination in the U.S. had a combined membership of 8,000 as of the 1970s. The church practices the teachings of Emmanuel Swedenborg (1688–1772), a scientist, seer, mystical philosopher, and religious writer.

Mary Henry (1841–1924), a spinster, worked as a seamstress for the wealthy U. P. Schenk family. No doubt this was the source for most of the silks and satins used in her quilt. One of the Schenk daughters suffered from allergies, and with Mary as her traveling companion spent the summers on Mackinac Island in northern Michigan. After the death of her parents, Mary lived with her sister and two brothers in a house on the banks of the Ohio River. Mrs. Hudelson, a grandniece of the quiltmaker, remembers the small English-style cottage with its flower gardens.

Tumbling Blocks

Tumbling Blocks. Pieced quilt. Mary M. Henry. Switzerland County, Indiana. Circa 1880. Silks and Satins. 80" × 73½". Collection of Charlotte Hudelson.

Mathursa Jane Crouse Craft.

Mathursa Jane Crouse Craft (1844–1922) and her daughter Lucretia Florence Craft Rissler Baumunk, maker of the Pine Burr quilt that follows, worked together to complete this commanding quilt, using fabrics from George Fox's general store in Reelsville. The nine-block style, indicative of quilts from an earlier era, belies the machine-inscribed date, "New Year's Eve 1889." Each tree is topped with a crown.

The quilting is by hand and machine with diagonal herringbone design in the nine pieced blocks and wreaths in the four plain blocks. The hand quilting is fine and even, boasting eleven stitches to the inch. The quilt has a four-inch border on two sides only.

Mathursa was a Putnam County native, and it was there that she and Daniel Craft married and they began a family of eleven children—five boys and six girls. The Crafts attended Big Walnut Baptist Church, and Mathursa and her daughters were active in the Ladies Aid Society.

Crowned Pine Tree

Pine Tree or Tree of Life. Pieced quilt. Made by Mathursa Jane Crouse Craft.
Buzzard's Roost, Putnam County, Indiana. 1889. Cotton. 79½" × 69". Collection of Peggy Potts.

Lucretia Craft Rissler Baumunk.

Pine Burr, a scrap pattern popular at the turn of the century, was made by Lucretia Craft (1868–1935) for her dowry. Her mother, Mathursa Jane Crouse Craft, who made the Pine Tree quilt above, probably helped with this quilt.

Pine Burr is a typical example of Craft family needlework from the excellent quality of the piecing and quilting to the completion date stitched into the corner. The vibrant colors used in Lucretia's quilt make it exciting to view. Even though Pine Burr is a scrap quilt, repeats of blues and yellows keep it from being too busy to the eye.

Pine Burr contains thirty pieced blocks and forty-nine plain blocks with two borders surrounding

the quilt. Lucretia did not rely only on her scrap bag, but also bought fabric from the Reelsville general store.

Quilted with nine stitches to the inch, the diagonal lines make a quiet background for the intricate, stylized pineapple motif found in the plain blocks. An inscription, "1898 quilted," tells when Lucretia finished her work.

Lucretia was nearly thirty by the time she married John Rissler. Following the birth of a daughter, the marriage ended in divorce. Lucretia later married John Baumunk and they resided in Buzzard's Roost in Putnam County.

Lucretia's Pine Burr Quilt

*Pine Burr. Pieced quilt. Made by Lucretia Florence Craft Rissler Baumunk.
Buzzard's Roost, Putnam County, Indiana. 1898. Cotton. 81¼" × 68". Collection of Peggy Potts.*

Mary Margaret White Critchfield.

Mary Margaret White (1870–1932) made her Triple Irish Chain quilt for her dowry, for she was in love and intending to marry. But fate had other plans. When her fiancé and another girl "got in trouble" and a child was on the way, Mary broke off the engagement.

When she was an "old maid" of thirty-eight, Mary married Richmond Critchfield at the Orange County Courthouse in 1908. They lived on a farm in rural Greenfield Township where she raised five orphaned children, two boys and three girls. They all attended Providence Christian Church.

An Irish Chain is an orderly quilt and Mary made it more so with the color changes she planned where the chains intersect. Embroidered on the quilt is the date of completion: "March 1888." The block repeats are constructed and quilted by hand with even stitches.

The quilt now belongs to a grandchild, the son of one of those five orphans she raised.

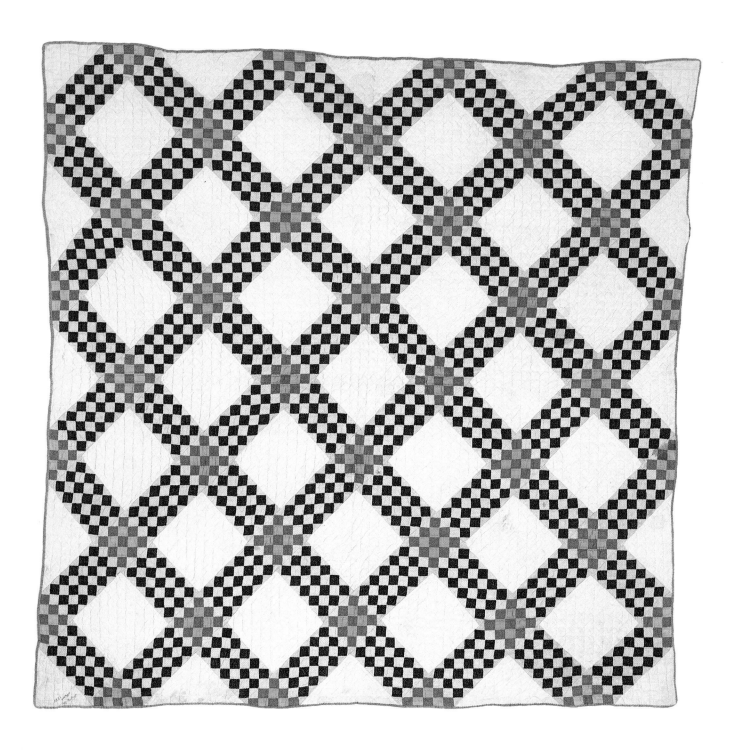

Mary Margaret's Triple Irish Chain

*Triple Irish Chain. Pieced quilt. Made by Mary Margaret White Critchfield.
Marengo, Crawford County, Indiana. 1888. Cotton. 71½" × 67¼". Collection of Royce Williams.*

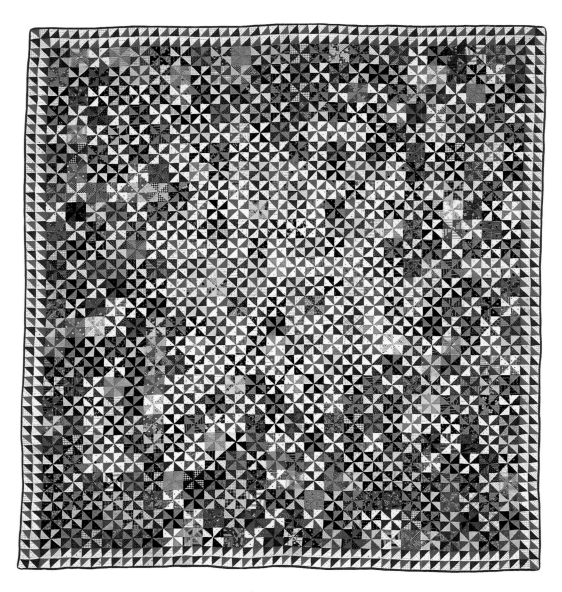

Maggie's Miniature Pinwheel

Miniature Pinwheel. Pieced scrap quilt. Maker Maggie Mellinger.
Fort Recovery, Ohio. Circa 1900. Cotton. 79" × 72". Collection of Janice Baumgartner.

Maggie Mellinger was a hired girl on the farm of George and Melissa Berkheimer near Fort Recovery, Ohio, when she pieced and quilted this stunning mini-pinwheel about 1900. Predominantly red, the quilt is made from multiple colored cotton scraps and contains 624 2¾" squares, each composed of four right angle triangles—the single template used for the quilt. There were 2,496 triangles in all.

Although Maggie made this quilt for her hope chest, she remained single her entire life. Quilt owner Janice Baumgartner, great-granddaughter of the Berkheimers, gives us this account:

Maggie worked for my great-grandparents until the early

1920s . . . and then went to a home for aged women, quite possibly the Emily Flinn Home in Marion, Indiana. I remember only vaguely visiting her a time or two. I was a very young child, maybe five years old.

I remember she had a single room for herself and she gave "surprises," usually candy, [quilt] pieces, or pretty hankies or small glass or china novelties which, I'm sorry to say, I never kept safely. We didn't go often, but she would always walk out on the grounds with us to say goodbye.

According to my Aunt Melissa Bond, who lived in this household until she graduated from high school in 1924 or 1925, and who died in 1988, Maggie spent all her extra time quilting, for her hope chest partially (this was true for the pinwheel quilt), but for family needs as well. I would assume she continued to quilt some after leaving the Berkheimer home.

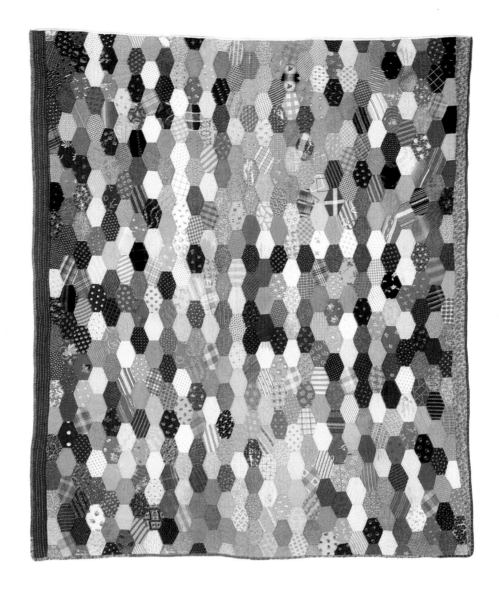

Ways of the World Quilt

Ways of the World. Pattern also called Coffin. Pieced quilt. Made by Cleon Brinegar.
Bloomington, Monroe County, Indiana. 1912–14. Cotton. 81" × 65". Collection of Edith Lawson.

Cleon Brinegar at the
time of her high school
graduation.

Cleon Brinegar (1895–1916) exchanged fabrics with neighborhood girl friends to make this charm quilt. They were also called beggar quilts, and the idea was for every piece in the single-template quilt to be a different fabric; however, duplicates have been found in Cleon's quilt. Cleon died at the age of twenty-one, and her quilt is now treasured by her sister.

Margurete Einspahr Sutton and Emerson Otto Sutton.

Margurete Einspahr Sutton (1878–1905), or "Mag" as her family and friends called her, learned dressmaking skills from her Aunt Mary in Chicago. Aunt Mary was described by the family as a perfectionist who did sewing for the Vanderbilt and Rothschild families.

The family tells us that Mag did lots of fancy sewing, including her own wedding dress and an identical one for her sister Emma's wedding. In addition, Mag was a talented musician who taught piano and organ before her marriage.

Margurete married Emerson Otto Sutton, a Lowell, Indiana, farmer twenty years her senior, on Christmas Eve 1903 in her parents' parlor. The Sutton farm, northwest of Lowell, had been settled in 1862. Part of the house had been moved from Mays in Rush County, Indiana, on a wagon pulled by oxen, but Emerson was building a new house for Margurete.

But Margurete would never live in her dream house. She died five days after giving birth to her only child, a son, Harold Morris Sutton, in May 1905. The present quilt owner is Harold's daughter-in-law.

Pinks and browns dominate this utility scrap quilt. Piecing was both by hand and machine. Plain blocks are used to emphasize the 195 stars formed in the sashing. The all-over quilting motif is commonly called Baptist Fan or Rainbow.

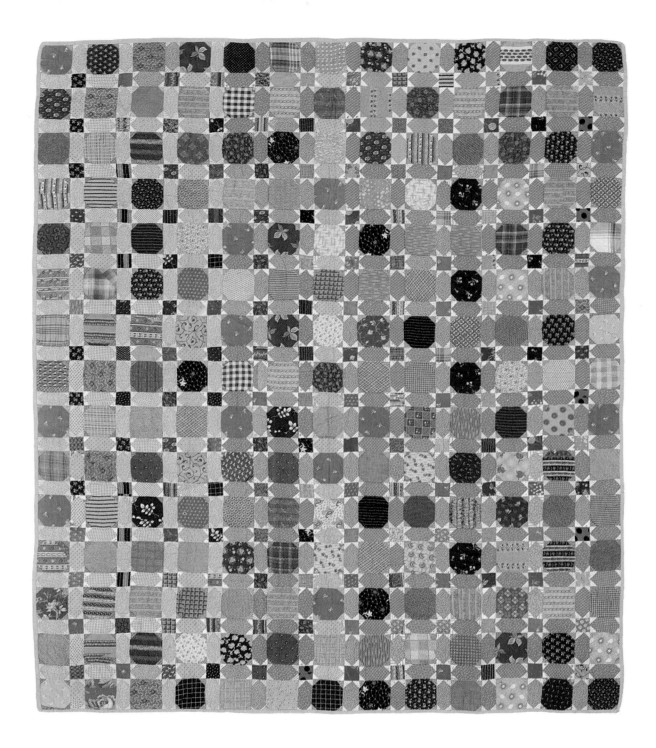

Margurete's Morning Star

Morning Star. Pieced quilt. Pieced by Margurete Einspahr Sutton.
Lowell, Lake County, Indiana. Circa 1900. Cotton. 76½" × 65".
Quilted 1940 by the Women's Circle of the First Church of Christ, Lowell, Indiana.
Collection of Carole D. Sutton.

Log Cabin Sunshine and Shadows

Log Cabin. Sunshine and Shadows variation. Pieced quilt. Made by Adelaide Malera Booher Cragun.
Whitestown, Boone County, Indiana. Circa 1900. Cotton and wool. 83½" × 73".
Collection of the Boone County Historical Society.

Adelaide Malera Booher Cragun (1857–1932) was one of twelve children. Quilts were a family project. The family recalls that Addie was assisted on this quilt by Emma Booher, Margaret Booher, Martha Booher, and Minnie Booher Tomlinson, although it is not known exactly what roles they all played. Addie was a housewife and the mother of three children, one son and twin daughters.

This Log Cabin is particularly effective because of the quiltmaker's use of color. She combined tan, black, and green, with purple centers. This Sunshine and Shadows variation uses 120 six-inch blocks. The border is not a striped fabric, but a most unusual and outstanding addition of twelve narrow, separate borders.

Martha Jane's Sampler

Sampler. Pieced quilt. Made by Martha Jane Richardson Sluss. Brummet's Creek, Monroe County, Indiana. Circa 1890. Quilted at a later date. Cotton. 78¼" × 66⅞". Collection of Dianna Lavon Durnal Kent.

Samplers have long been a learning tool in all forms of needlework from embroidery to quiltmaking. This sampler was made in the 1890s by Martha Jane Richardson Sluss (1871–1918) of Brummett's Creek in Monroe County, Indiana.

It is not a planned, formal quilt; and it utilized old cotton clothing scraps as well as some new scraps. There is a wonderful array of hand-pieced blocks of various sizes and complexity. Family history relates that one small nine-patch block in the lower right-hand corner was made by Martha Jane's daughter, Mary Catherine Sluss Spriggs, when she was five or six years old, and was set into the "big" quilt by her mother. Her nine-patch is quite a contrast to the outstanding Mariner's Compass block in the center of the quilt.

The current owner is the great-great-granddaughter of Martha Jane.

Flags of the World

Tobacco premium flags. Medallion novelty quilt. Maker unknown. Fort Wayne, Allen County, Indiana. Circa 1924. Cotton. 77½" × 64". Collection of Robert Parker.

"Flags of the World" given as premiums by to-bacco companies have been set together for this novelty quilt. One larger United States flag dominates the center. Forty-eight stars are found in the U.S. flag, giving an important clue that the date of the quilt is early twentieth century.

The premiums, called flannels, were collected as baseball cards are today. This particular top also contains flannels of sports activities, colleges, flow-ers, etc. They are set together with a buttonhole embroidery stitch which has caught the back at the same time to stabilize the whole. No batting was used.

Tobacco premiums featuring famous people have also been used in crazy quilts. An important geogra-phy or history lesson may be learned from studying these quilts.

College Pennants

College pennants. All-over crazy quilt. Pressed method. Made by Elizabeth Ann Rogers Berry.
Monon, White County, Indiana. Circa 1914. Felt. 75" × 57". Collection of Winifred Berry Starrett.

When her niece, Iris Boughman, left for Oklahoma State University, Elizabeth Ann Rogers Berry presented her with a college comforter of pennants for her dormitory room. Schools represented range from Indiana and Purdue Universities to Valparaiso College and Rensselaer Polytechnic Institute. The Boughman family and their friends had collected the pennants as souvenirs in their travels; Elizabeth made the quilt by featherstitching them together. Two of the felt pennants are dated 1913, and many depict campus scenes or the school mascot. The backing is cotton sateen fabric that has been folded over to the front side to bind off the bed cover.

Lucretia Ann Alexander Campbell (1862–1957), shown with her grandchildren Marilyn L. Cripe and Buddie Cripe. Photograph courtesy of Marilyn L. Cripe Wilson, from *Annie's Quilt* (privately published, 1987).

Signature quilts were a popular way of raising money for causes and organizations at the turn of the century. Annie Campbell decided to help the Salem Methodist Church build its new sanctuary by making a signature quilt. She embroidered approximately six hundred names on this quilt, sold chances on it for a drawing, and raised $350. The winner of the drawing was to have been the new quilt owner, but the signatories decided to give it back to Annie.

On the quilt in addition to the names is the inscription, "Salem Church 1875–1909." Annie quilted her fundraiser with maroon thread in the ditch or seam. Solid colors of blue, black, tan, and maroon cotton have been used in the quilt top. It has cotton batting and a cotton print backing which has been folded over to the top for the binding.

Annie loved the poems of Hoosier poet James Whitcomb Riley and knew them all by heart. She loved to give readings, a popular pastime in the early years of this century, and was excellent with dialects.

Visitors to the Cass County Historical Society, where it is often on display, like to search Annie's quilt for names of relatives or friends. A booklet about the quilt was written and published by Marilyn Wilson, Annie's granddaughter.

Annie's Fan Signature Quilt

*Fan signature quilt. Family name, Annie's Quilt. Pieced, appliqued, and embroidered.
Made by Lucretia Ann "Annie" Alexander Campbell. Walton, Cass County, Indiana. 1909.
Cotton. 87" × 85". Collection of the Cass County Historical Society.*

Album Quilt

Album quilt. Maker unknown. Location unknown. 1886. Cotton. 78" × 64½".
Collection of James Sanders.

This pieced quilt has signatures, sentiments, and drawings in India ink. It was made for a Reverend Cockrun at the time of his retirement. Not much is known about it, but possibly it was a Ladies Aid Society quilt. Dated 1886.

Signature Quilt

Signature quilt, Red Church House pattern. Pieced quilt.
Made by the Ladies Aid Society of the New Highland Christian Church. Terre Haute, Vigo County, Indiana.
1898. Cotton. 80" × 70". Collection of the Vigo County Historical Society.

Mable Nevin Baer Kemper shows a detail of the Dayton Methodist Church Ladies Aid Society quilt.

The Ladies were talented; the embroidery on both quilts is excellent, as is the workmanship. The 10½ inch squares of muslin were embroidered in red thread, and the sixty blocks were constructed in a "quilt as you go" method. There is no batting, but a layer of fabric was used as filler.

Blocks included names of church members, early settlers of Dayton, and previous pastors of the church. There are 886 names in all. The quilt was purchased by Mrs. Nevin Baer (sixteen Baer family names appear on the quilt). Mrs. Baer gave it to her daughter Mable Nevin Baer Kemper who kept it until her death. Mrs. Kemper's children, Floyd Kemper, Dorothy Seal, and Lillian Reppy, donated it to the Tippecanoe County Historical Association in memory of their mother.

Before the 1891 and 1908 quilts were placed in their new homes, Jesse Hulon Wheeler, historian for the Dayton Church, compiled all the information available about the quilts into a booklet. Thanks to his dedication, the information has been preserved.

The Ladies Aid Society of the Methodist Church of Dayton was active in helping the church to raise money for building and refurbishing by making quilts like this one. They placed names on the quilt for five cents each and then sold the finished quilt. In a letter written in 1979, Mrs. Della Dunwoody, one of the oldest living church members, said, "It was a custom to make these named quilts for sale at the annual Harvest Bazaar."

The center block is twenty-one inches square. A Bible, surrounded by leaves and leaning against a large cross, is open to 2 Corinthians 9:7. "Every man according as he purposeth in his heart, so let him give; not grudgingly, or of necessity; for God loveth a cheerful giver." The date, 1891, is shown in this block with three names: Mrs. L. Boyles, Mrs. M. Lentz, and Mrs. E. Osenbach. A second similar red and white signature quilt dated 1908 is owned by the church. That quilt says "Ladies Aid Society" in the center block with a similar Bible and cross design.

The old Dayton Methodist Church in Tippecanoe County (photograph courtesy of the *Lafayette Journal and Courier*).

The Ladies Aid Society Quilt

Signature Blocks. Embroidered quilt. Made by the Ladies Aid Society of the Dayton Methodist Church. Dayton, Tippecanoe County, Indiana. 1891. Cotton. 84" × 84". Collection of the Tippecanoe County Historical Association

Americus quilters in 1917. Front two rows, left to right: Susan Murphy, Elizie Thorpe, Belle Dice, Queny Dubes, Carrie Eckenrode (founder); back: Goldie Swoden, Dora Merkel, Susan Deboy, Mary Schnepp, Della Dubes.

LADIES AID SOCIETY QUILTS

Quilting has always played a role in women's lives out of necessity, but it also provides an opportunity to spend time working and chatting with friends. All over Indiana, groups of women still meet to quilt together, sharing their life stories around the frame. Often the group has a philanthropic purpose as well.

One such charitable group had its inception when four women got together to quilt on December 1, 1887, at the log house of Nettie (Mrs. Henry) Ilgenfritz in Wea, Tippecanoe County. A second meeting was held the following month. Thus began the Willing Workers of Wea, now called Wea Willing Workers or WWW. Charter members were Mrs. Ilgenfritz, Jennie (Mrs. Lemmuel) Hudlow, Jane (Mrs. Corb) Huffman, Mrs. Rose Brubaker, Maggie (Mrs. Ira) Roudebush, and Mrs. John McCoy. They paid dues of five cents per meeting or sixty cents per year. Early members recalled tying the quilting frames to their horses' saddles when they went to meetings. Around 1910 the frames were transported courtesy of Mrs. Jane Stidham's horse and buggy.

Meetings were held at the homes of members, and usually included a noon meal. In their hundred-plus years of service, the WWW have made clothing, linens, and curtains as well as quilts which were presented to disaster victims and to the Cary Home for Children, Home Hospital, and St. Elizabeth Hospital in Lafayette. WWW raised money to buy materials and fabrics by serving lunches at sales and auctions in the area and by quilting for hire. In 1932, during the Depression, annual dues had to be reduced to twenty-five cents a year. Because of shortages and rationing during World War II, members brought their own coffee and sugar to meetings.

Americus quilters celebrating their sixtieth anniversary in 1975. Seated, left to right: Edith Klaiber, Mabel Tobor, Emma Jacot, Bertha Buck, Sadie Titus, Letha Nelson, Sue Schnepp, Barbara Watson, Lena Bieber, Gertie Reynolds, Laura Schnepp, Sylvia Sanders. Standing: Elma Daugherty, Eileen Titus, Juanita McClonahan, Mildred Smith, Effie Emerich, Eva Boyce, Ethel Lamb.

Mary Jane Stacker has the distinction of being a third-generation member of WWW: she follows in the footsteps of her mother, Irene Hefner Emdee, and both grandmothers, Mary Emdee and Jane Hefner.

The Americus Ladies Aid was organized in March 1915 with twelve members when Carrie Eckenrode of Battleground in Tippecanoe County invited some women to her house. The purpose of the quilting group was to raise money for the Americus Union Church. Meetings were held in members' homes; a quilting fee of one cent per yard of thread was charged. In those days the cost of having a top quilted ranged from five to six dollars. The group has always lent a helping hand with bedcovers and other items for needy families and disaster victims, and with monetary donations to charitable organizations.

In 1944 the group's name was changed to the Americus Quilting Club. Support of the church was no longer its main purpose, and membership was open to anyone. The group first met at members' homes, later at the Tippecanoe Battleground Park Museum, and now convenes at the Battleground United Methodist Church. Their fee for quilting has escalated to fifteen cents per yard of quilting thread. It is estimated they have stitched over 135,000 yards of thread into more than four hundred quilts. Americus gives quilting demonstrations at schools, shopping centers, stores, and festivals, and since 1975 has hosted an annual quilt show. During the governorship of Robert Orr, the group was honored to receive a request from Mrs. Orr for twin bed quilts for a bedroom in the Governor's Mansion. Upon completion of the quilts, members were entertained at a luncheon at the mansion.

The Americus Quilting Club meets on the second and fourth Thursdays of each month. Members quilt from 10:00 A.M. to 3:30 P.M., breaking for a potluck lunch at noon.

Mary Zelinda Robinson lived all her life in the rural community of Danville in Hendricks County, Indiana. Born March 11, 1829, she was married on her forty-first birthday, in 1870, to James Wilson Robinson. She attended the Danville Presbyterian Church, became the mother of eight children—seven boys and one girl—and died in 1920, at ninety-one.

It is unknown whether any of her sons fought in the Spanish-American war, but some may have been the right age. Her quilt was made for the Red Cross Benefit Auction in 1898 and was purchased by her oldest son. It has become a treasured family heirloom along with a poem she wrote for the occasion (reprinted below), and is passed from one generation to the next by way of the oldest son in the family. The present owner is Mary Zelinda's great-great-great-grandson.

The appliqued stars seem to dance at random among the stripes. Not so; all but two stars have been placed with the inside point precisely lining up with the seam of the red and white stripes.

The blocks are sewn together in vertical strips, joined by red and white striped sashing, meant to suggest the stripes of Old Glory. The stars are applied with a buttonhole stitch and quilted with a pentagon inside them. All other quilting follows the pieced shapes, eight stitches to the inch. Binding is straight applied and there is no filling. The quilt has apparently never been used or washed, and retains all of its original brilliance.

THE LOYALTY QUILT
MARY ZELINDA ROBINSON

The quilt is an emblem
Of loyalty true
With the Red Cross encircled
By the National blue.
A token of purity, sacrifice too
And manifests plainly
What a woman can do
Hurrah for the Red Cross
The red, white and blue.

The stars and stripes
Are a token of love
For Freedom and Justice
Transcribed from above
The Red Cross combined
With all loyalty true
Three cheers for the Red Cross
And the red, white and blue.

Hurrah for Old Glory
The flag of the free
An emblem of sacrifice
For you and for me
Our brave boys are fighting
For victory true
Hurrah for the dear boys
Of red, white and blue.

Mary Zelinda's Loyalty Quilt

Loyalty Quilt. Pieced quilt. Made by Mary Zelinda Robinson. Danville, Hendricks County, Indiana. 1898.
Cotton. 94½" × 79½". Collection of Brad Parker.

Marie Webster: Indiana's Gift to American Quilts

Cuesta Benberry

4Marie Daugherty Webster has earned a distinguished position among America's quilt notables. A recounting of her extraordinary contributions reveals a multifaceted woman. As a pioneering quilt designer, a superb quiltmaker, an innovative entrepreneur, and a major influence on the direction of twentieth century quilt design, she left her mark on our times. More than three quarters of a century after her first designs were published, evidence of Marie Webster's continued impact on America's quilts can be found.

Marie Daugherty was born in Wabash, Indiana, on July 15, 1859, to Minerva H. (Lumaree) and Josiah Scott Daugherty. Both the Lumaree and Daugherty families were prominent in the community.

Although Marie inherited her stature from her mother, she closely resembled her father. With her classic features and soft voice, she was very elegant and ladylike, prim and gracious, according to those who knew her.

Marie married George W. Webster, Jr., a business acquaintance of her banker father's, on Valentine's Day 1884. In 1885 they had a son whom they named Lawrence for Marie's younger brother. The Webster, Jr. family soon moved to Marion, where George's family resided. George and Marie collected

art in their world-wide travels and displayed it in their Victorian home at 926 South Washington Street. George died in 1938. Marie continued to live in Marion until 1942 when she moved to Princeton, New Jersey, to live with her son, his wife, Jeanette, and their two daughters. Marie died at Princeton in 1956 at the age of ninety-seven.

National attention was drawn to Marie Webster when four of her applique quilts appeared as color sketches in the January 1911 issue of *The Ladies Home Journal*, America's leading women's magazine. At the time, the magazine was published in the large 16¼" × 11½" format. The soft pastel colors in the beautiful quilts called Pink Rose, Iris, Snowflake, and Windblown Tulip were presented on a full page under the title "The New Patchwork Quilt," with Webster's byline. It must have been a coup for the magazine; the quilts were so new and so different from what were generally accepted as typical American quilts. In that era, quilts meant replicas of nineteenth century quilt concepts: vivid palettes, frequent flamboyance, and intricately designed motifs.

Webster's new designs were models of restrained elegance, simplicity, and quiet beauty. The contrast between old and new was never greater. *The Ladies Home Journal* quickly followed up with an August 1911 presentation, "The New Patchwork Cushion" by Marie D. Webster, featuring nine appliqued

Marie Daugherty Webster (1859–1956).
Photograph courtesy of the
Indianapolis Museum of Art.

cushions in her same design mode. The cushion patterns were readily adaptable to block patterns for full-sized bed quilts.

Four more quilts—Poppy, Sunflower, Morning Glories, and Dogwood—graced the *Journal*'s January 1912 issue under the heading "The New Patchwork Flower Quilt" by Marie D. Webster. The August 1912 issue featured six small quilts—Bedtime, Sunbonnet Lassies, Wild Rose, Golden Butterflies and Pansies, Morning Glory, and Daisy—in Webster's article, "The Baby's Patchwork Quilt." Patterns for the quilts could be obtained by writing to Mrs. Webster in care of the magazine at the Philadelphia address. Pattern diagrams were also printed in the magazine's supplementary needlework sales catalog.[1]

Further study of Marie Webster's contributions to the *Journal* indicates a break between 1912 and 1915. During this interval she was at work on her landmark book. In October 1915, however, the *Journal* published "A Rose Patchwork Bedroom," displaying an entire matching bedroom furnishings ensemble, including bed quilt, cushion, table cover, bed pillow, scarf or nap pillow, chair cover, and a bureau, chiffonier, or table scarf. Although it was not illustrated, Webster suggested picking up the vine motif for use as a curtain border.

Her floral basket quilt in the September 1927 *Journal* article entitled "Pink Dogwoods in Applique" was just as lovely as her earlier quilts, if not more so. And her 1930 and 1931 articles for the widely circulated needlework journal *Needlecraft* denote no diminution of her ability to produce items that had appeal, even though by this time Webster was seventy years old.[2]

Historical accuracy demands that Marie Webster's role in bringing a new look to twentieth-century quilts not be overstated. There is no claim that she accomplished this feat singlehanded. Prior to the publication of any of her works, evidence can be found linking other sources to realistic floral portrayals, juvenile-themed baby quilts, subdued pastel colors, a revolt against Victorian ornateness, and an espousal of delicate designs in appliqued quilts.[3] However, because of her affiliation with the most prominent women's magazine of the day and the resulting national exposure, Webster became the personification of the new look in quilts. Undeniably she did popularize a trend.

When Marie Webster wrote the first history of quilts, *Quilts, Their Story and How to Make Them* (1915), she was filling a need. In it she wrote:

Although the quilt is one of the most familiar and necessary articles in our households, its story is yet to be told. In spite of its universal use and intimate connection with our

Marie Webster lived at 926 S. Washington Street in Marion in this three-story Victorian house. The top floor has eyebrow-type window dormers. The front porch has six white columns and extends the full width of the gray-painted house. According to local folklore, the house was constructed with lumber from the defunct York Inn, a resort operated in the gas boom era, and the interior woodwork was imported from Germany's Black Forest.

lives, its past is a mystery which—at most—can only be partially unravelled.

Webster's global view of patchwork and quilting and their ancient antecedents made hers an excellent first quilt history text. Her book was illustrated with both color and black and white plates. With the exception of the frontispiece, "Indiana Wreath," the color plates were original Marie Webster designs. The black and white plates were of antique quilts, often owned by her Midwestern friends and acquaintances. One of them is illustrated in this chapter. Several of the quilts pictured in the black and white plates were later donated to the Art Institute of Chicago.[4]

Although they are not illustrated, the more than 450 patterns on her List of Quilt Names are indicative of quilt names in common use prior to 1915. A 1960 study of Webster's list determined that it was probably a combination of folkloric titles and ones acquired from previously published sources. The published sources she researched were The Ladies Art Company; *Pictorial Review Magazine, House Beautiful, Woman's Home Companion, Woman's World Magazine, Ladies Home Journal*, and possibly a few farm papers. A 1913 issue of a widely distributed magazine referred to one pattern as Abolition Rose instead of using Webster's listed name, Radical Rose; another, called I Will and I Won't, was listed by Webster as Robbing Peter to Pay Paul. It was ob-

viously not the source she used for her list of pattern names. Her bibliography indicates the scarcity of historical needlework references available for Webster's research. In that regard, *The Art of Needle-Work from the Earliest Ages*, edited by the Countess of Wilton (1840), may have been especially beneficial to Webster's studies. It is also apparent that much of her work was based on primary research. Today one occasionally hears criticisms of the Webster book's lack of conformity with present standards for historical writing. It should be remembered that in 1915 when she wrote it, quilts were considered colorful or charming or quaint, but a woman's household chore nonetheless and thus not a fitting scholarly topic. Yet it is evident that the book was a research-based text.

Quilts, Their Story and How to Make Them has gone through several editions, and with each edition there have been changes, additions, and subtractions. The editions published by Doubleday, Page (1915, 1926) apparently had Marie Webster's cooperation and approval. Doubleday, Doran issued an edition dated 1928; Tudor published a 1948 edition, and Gale Research's version, minus any color plates, appeared in 1972. Until 1929 the Webster book was the only hard-cover quilt history text available, and was regarded as the authoritative one. Numerous newspapers and magazines reviewed it favorably and based their own quilt history articles on data gleaned from it.

Marie Webster formed the Practical Patchwork

There is nothing difficult about applique—painstaking is the chief requisite; and she who may lay claim to this qualification, even though a novice in decorative stitchery, will be able to produce a quilt as perfect in every way as can be made by any long-time expert . . . one has only to hem or blindstitch the flowers and stems in place, using fine self-color sewing-thread and taking stitches so tiny that a magnifying-glass would be required to discover them!

—Marie Webster

Company, a mail-order pattern cottage industry, about 1920. Women working in the Webster home in Marion cut patches from colored tissue paper and pasted them onto a background to create a model of the quilt block, or one-fourth of the baby quilt, whatever was required. Another Practical Patchwork Company innovation was a drawn-to-size pattern printed on a draftsman's type blueprint paper with full instructions.

In addition to paper patterns, the company offered boxed cloth kits, basted quilt tops, and, for an extra fee, fully completed quilts of any design in the Webster inventory. The work of making completed quilts was farmed out to quilters in several locations. Information about the patterns was disseminated by advertisements, and the Practical Patchwork Company also issued successive editions of an illustrated catalogue, *Quilts and Spreads*. Archival materials pertaining to Marie Webster indicate that her quilts, kits, and patterns were also sold by Eleanor Beard Inc., Hedgelands Studio, Hardinsburg, Kentucky; A. M. Caden (the Caden sisters), Lexington, Kentucky; and the Marshall Field Company, Chicago.

In the early twentieth century, many quilt patterns from commercial sources were issued under the name of the company, or often under a pseudonym. Marie Webster has been characterized as the first professional quilt designer known by her own name. She led the way for those who later embarked on various entrepreneurial careers in quilts, including Anne Orr, Carlie Sexton, Mary McElwain, Ruby Short McKim, Emma S. Tyrrell, Orinne Johnson, Florence LaGanke *aka* "Nancy Page," and Marion Cheever Whiteside.

Indiana seems to have been a choice location for early quilt business operations such as the Esther O'Neill Company in Indianapolis and the Wilkinson Art Company of Ligonier. Both of these Indiana quilt ventures were concurrent with the Practical Patchwork Company, and the O'Neill Company's origins predate it.

By offering paper patterns, quilt kits, basted quilts, and completed quilts, the Practical Patchwork Company reached a wide range of potential customers. The less diversified Esther O'Neill Company sold stamped quilt kits to be completed. The Wilkinson sisters, Rosalie and Ona, proprietors of the Wilkinson Art Company, sold kits and completed handmade quilts targeted to the luxury market.[5]

A fascinating aspect of the Marie D. Webster story is the extent to which her designs were reproduced by other pattern producers. Some effort is necessary today to trace the patterns to their creator. Surprisingly, Webster's first sponsor, *The Ladies Home Journal*, reprinted her Wreath of Roses in 1933, renaming it Wild Rose and omitting any attribution to the designer. The Wreath of Roses pattern was also featured as Rose Spray in *The Indiana Farmer* and as Circle of Roses in *The Household Journal*. Neither of the magazines gave credit to Webster.

Her unusual French Baskets design acquired new titles, Ivory Baskets from Mrs. Danner's Quilts and Basket of Daisies from *The Household Journal*. As examples of unchanged titles, Dogwood by Webster became Dogwood by Aunt Martha's Studio and #29 Dogwood by Mountain Mist/Stearns and Foster. *The Chicago Tribune*'s Nancy Cabot did manage a slight alteration with the name Dogwood Beauty.

Possibly because of their intricacy, certain Webster patterns proved resistant to duplication. Present evidence indicates that only the Mary McElwain Quilt Shop copied Webster's Rainbow pattern, presenting it as Spring Bouquet. Mrs. Danner's Quilts' Rose with Watermelon Border duplicated Webster's Pink Rose/American Beauty Rose. Trailing Tulips was the name applied by both *Capper's Weekly* and Mrs. Danner's Quilts for Webster's May Tulips.

The copying and sharing of quilt patterns has always been a tradition among quiltmakers. Yet it is unfortunate when one commercial enterprise appropriates and publishes without attribution the original works of another. An adverse effect in this case was the loss of all connection with the Webster name for some of the quilt designs she created.

A study was made to determine if Marie Webster's designs were truly original or if they, too, were copies of previous designers' works. No instances of outright copying could be discovered, but a very few designs did seem to be influenced by earlier concepts. There is, however, a difference between outright copying and being inspired by another designer. It seems certain that the greater proportion of Marie Webster's designs can be termed original, with only a minimal influence from earlier works.

The Indianapolis Museum of Art owns ten original Marie Webster quilts donated by Jeanette Thurber in memory of her mother-in-law. Mrs. Thurber was married to Marie Webster's son, Lawrence.

The differences between nineteenth century quilts and quilts made in the first half of the twentieth century were most apparent in those that were appliqued. It is undeniable that Marie Webster was a principal force for change in the look of twentieth century appliqued quilts. We can cite few other persons who have had a similar influence on the aesthetics of twentieth century quilts, or the recording of global quilt history, or who displayed the entrepreneurial verve of Marie Daugherty Webster, Indiana's gift to American quilts.

NOTES

1. *The Ladies Home Journal Embroidery Book*, vol. 8, no. 13 (New York: Home Pattern Company Publishers), p. 74. The Marie Webster patterns, entitled "Designs for Patchwork and Applique for the Nursery," were #14529, Sunbonnet Babies, Bedtime Kiddies; #44374, Morning Glory, Dogwood; #14386, cushions—Rose Vine, Iris, Basket.

2. The September 1930 *Needlecraft—The Magazine of Home Arts* (Augusta, Maine) contained two articles by Marie

D. Webster: "The May Tulip in Applique," p. 6, and "The Cherokee Rose," p. 25.

3. See for example *Latest Designs in Embroidery: Catalog of Fancy Work* (St. Louis, Mo.: Ladies Art Co., n.d. [ca. 1910]); *Colonial Patchwork: Quilts, Coverlets, Etc.* (New York: Charles E. Bentley, 1916); *Martha Washington Patch Work Quilt Book* (St. Louis, Mo.: St. Louis Fancy Work Co., n.d. [ca. 1914]).

4. Mildred Davison, *American Quilts* (Chicago: Art Institute, 1966). The quilts are #9 Charter Oak (1835); #21 Pumpkin Blossom (1848: this quilt was listed as Whig Rose in Webster's book); #22 Poinsettia (ca. 1850); and #28 Pineapple (ca. 1852). They are the gift of Emma B. Hodge, and each has a 1919 classification number, indicating the year of donation.

5. For more information on the Wilkinson Company, see chapter 5. *Esther O'Neill Designs* (quilt pattern sales catalogue, 205 State Life Building, Indianapolis, Indiana, n.d.). Maude Bass Brown, "Dollar Signs in Quilting," *The Modern Priscilla* (October 1920), p. 3.

BIBLIOGRAPHY

Archives, Indianapolis Museum of Art.
Benberry, Cuesta. "Marie D. Webster Quilt Patterns, Part 1." *Nimble Needle Treasures Magazine*, vol. 7 no. 2 (1975), pp. 1–4.
———. "The 20th Century's First Quilt Revival, Part 2." *Quilter's Newsletter Magazine*, no. 115 (September 1979), pp. 25–26+.
Dunton, William Rush. *Old Quilts*. Catonsville, Md.: Self-published, 1946.
Files, Marion Public Library.
Files, *Marion Chronicle* and *Marion Chronicle-Tribune*.
Hall, Carrie, and Rose Kretsinger. *The Romance of the Patchwork Quilt in America*. Caldwell, Idaho: Caxton Printers, 1935.
Interview, Isabel Campbell of Marion, Indiana.
Interview, Residents of the Warfel House of Marion, Indiana.
Marton, Gwen, and Joe Cunningham. *American Beauties: Rose and Tulip Quilts*. Paducah, Ky.: American Quilter's Society, 1988).
Webster, Marie D. *Quilts, Their Story and How to Make Them*. New York: Doubleday, Page, 1915.
———. *Quilts and Spreads* (sales catalogue). Marion, Ind.: Marie D. Webster, n.d.
———. *Quilts and Spreads* (sales catalogue). Marion, Ind.: Practical Patchwork Co., n.d.
———. "The New Patchwork Quilt." *Ladies Home Journal* (Philadelphia: January 1911).
———. "The New Patchwork Cushion." *Ladies Home Journal* (Philadelphia: August 1911).
———. "The Flower Patchwork Quilt." *Ladies Home Journal* (Philadelphia: January 1912).
———. "The Baby's Patchwork Quilt." *Ladies Home Journal* (Philadelphia: August 1912).
———. "A Rose Patchwork Bedroom." *Ladies Home Journal* (Philadelphia: October 1915).
———. "The Coverlet and the Cushion." *Ladies Home Journal* (Philadelphia: February 1918).
———. "Pink Dogwood in Applique." *Ladies Home Journal* (Philadelphia: September 1927).
———. "The Cherokee Rose Quilt." *Needlecraft—The Magazine of Home Arts* (Augusta, Maine: September 1930).
———. "The May Tulip in Applique." *Needlecraft—The Magazine of Home Arts* (Augusta, Maine: May 1931).
Wilton, Countess of. *The Art of Needle-Work from the Earliest Ages*. London: Henry Colburn Pub., 1840.
Woodard, Thomas K. and Blanche Greenstein. *Twentieth Century Quilts, 1900–1950*. New York: E. P. Dutton, 1988.

Marie Webster Poppy

Poppy. Appliqued medallion style quilt. Maker and location unknown. Circa 1920.
Cotton sateen. 84" × 72". Collection of Lynn Demaree.

Marie Webster's Poppy design was the epitome of Art Nouveau elegance. This version was constructed of glazed and polished cotton, primarily cotton sateen. The spread was deliberately constructed for a poster bed, with cutouts for the posts. The quilting is a very fine fourteen stitches to the inch. Although owner Lynn Demaree doesn't know who the quilt-maker was, she believes the quilt was made in Connecticut in the early part of the century. This Webster pattern was first published in *The Ladies Home Journal* in the January 1912 issue.

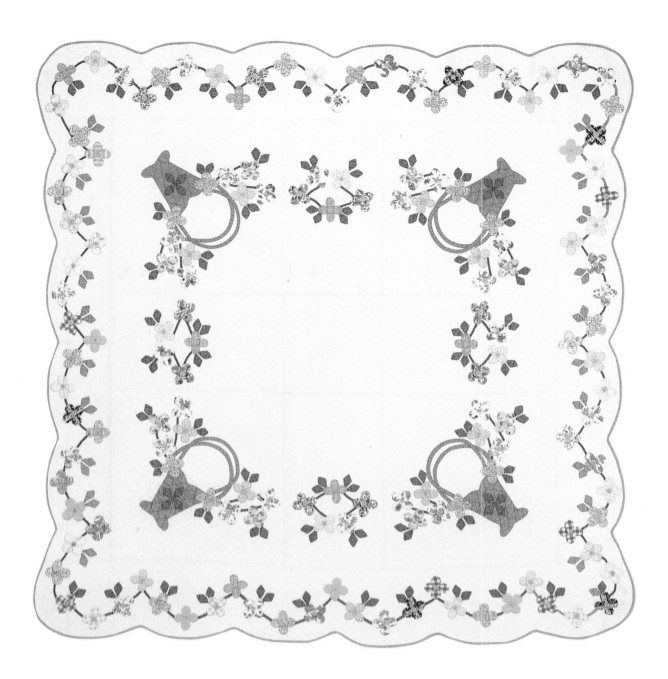

Flower Basket

Flower Basket. Appliqued quadrant. Made by Nola Skinner Collins. Kennard, Henry County, Indiana. Circa 1930. Cotton. 82¾" × 75". Collection of Mary Lou Hessey.

A Quaker woman from Michigan, Nola Skinner Collins (1876–1964) was living at Kennard in Henry County when she worked on this quilt about 1930. The pattern is a Marie Webster design that was featured in the September 1927 *Ladies Home Journal*.

Nola chose green for the baskets and pastels for the flowers—typical colors for the time. Skilled with her sewing machine, Nola used machine applique on all her flowers.

Stella Grace Humphrey Mather.

Stella Grace Humphrey Mather (1878–1955), of Springfield, Ohio, made this Pink Dogwood in a Basket sometime before 1943 as a gift for Betty Ellen Mather, who married Stella's grandson, Jack. Betty Mather still owns the quilt. Inscribed on it, in addition to the owner's name, date, and place, is a Bible verse: "My grace is sufficient for thee" (2 Cor. 12:9).

The design was the last Marie Webster pattern published in *The Ladies Home Journal* (September 1927). Its quadrant style was also popular during the first half of the nineteenth century. The appliqued shapes are outlined with feathers. The quilt edges are gracefully scalloped with rounded corners.

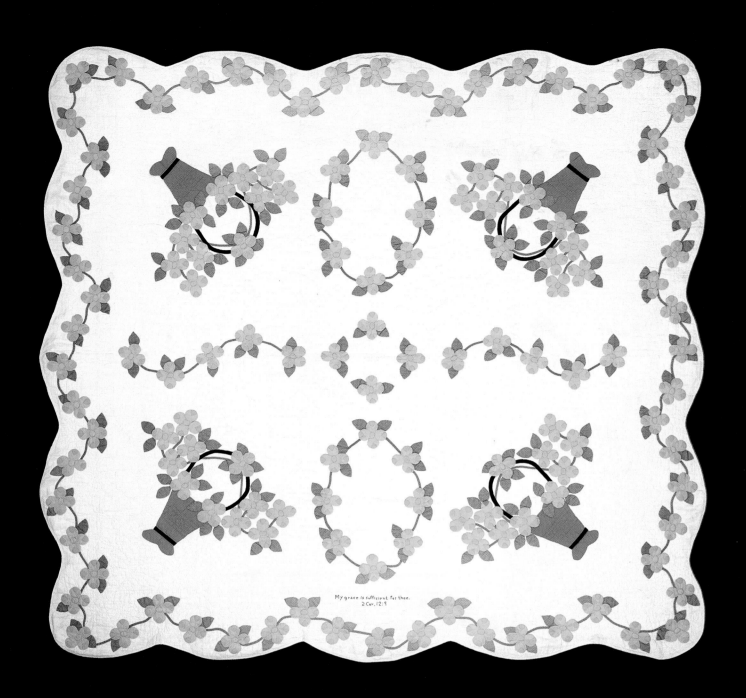

My grace is sufficient for thee.
2 Cor. 12:9

Pink Dogwood

Pink Dogwood. Appliqued quadrant quilt. Made by Stella Grace Humphrey Mather. Springfield, Ohio. Circa 1930. Cotton. 83½" × 81½". Collection of Betty Ellen Mather.

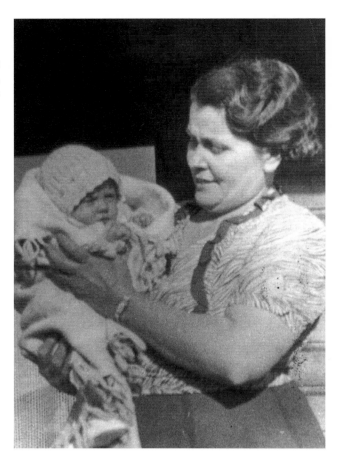

Cleo Eva Antrim Durkes, shown with her first granddaughter, Janet Durkes Lippold.

Constructed of purple, green, white, and yellow fabrics, this quilt was made by Carolyn Schroer's mother, Cleo Eva Antrim Durkes (1895–1973), and her grandmother, Martha Smith Antrim, in the early 1930s. The family lived at Converse in Miami County, Indiana.

May Tulips was Pattern No. 4504N in *Needlecraft—The Magazine of Home Arts*. Patterns could be ordered from any Needlecraft Club-Raiser, or by mail, postpaid from Needlecraft Magazine, Augusta, Maine. An article describing the quilt appeared in the May 1931 issue.

Another Marie Webster design, this quilt pattern shows graceful placement of the tulips in nine blocks, each 22″ × 27″, edged by scalloped borders. On her version of this pattern, Cleo chose to reverse the direction of the border tulips. Instead of facing the center of the quilt, they face the edges.

Cleo and Martha were expert needlewomen—there are twelve to fourteen stitches per inch in the quilting. Together they made enough quilts so that each of Cleo's seven children received two each. Carolyn chose her quilts in 1959, the year she was married. This one had been made before she was born.

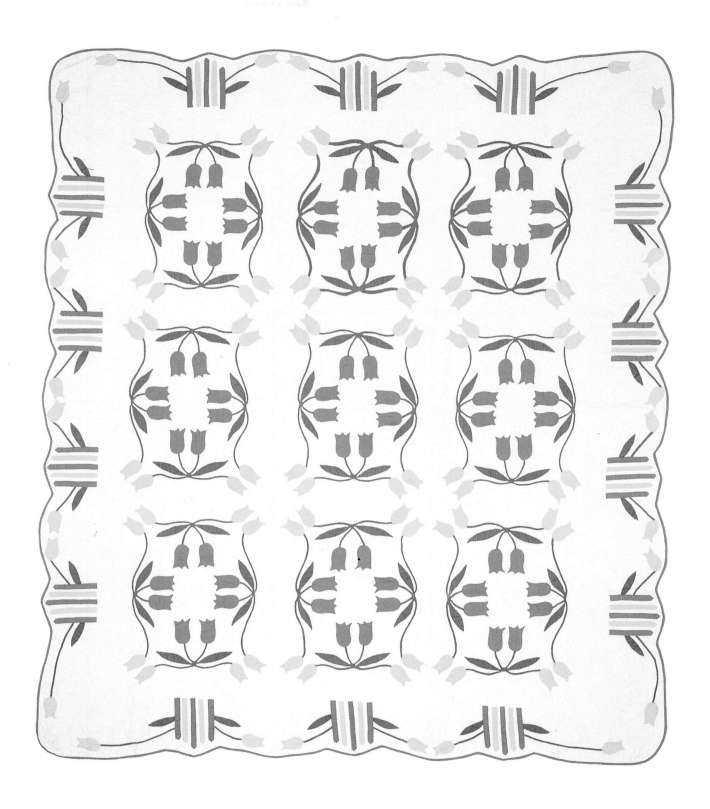

May Tulips

May Tulips. Appliqued block repeat. Made by Cleo Eva Antrim Durkes and Martha Smith Antrim. Converse, Miami County, Indiana. Circa 1930. Cotton. 88¾" × 75¾". Collection of Carolyn Schroer.

This is one of the early quilts pictured in *Quilts, Their Story and How to Make Them*, by Marie Webster (1915). It is identified as an "Original Floral Design"; however, Mrs. Webster set the date of the quilt as circa 1825, made in Southern Indiana, while the family believes it to be circa 1850. An examination of the fabrics shows that both could have been correct; the quilt top could have been made about 1850 from older fabrics dating back to the 1820s or 1830s.

The wonderful old sampler has graceful and unique appliqued blocks, skillfully done and set on point, with white blocks separating the appliques. The later quilting was done in outline of the appliqued shapes and feathered wreaths in the white spacing blocks.

The finishing border swags or festoons are decorated with cockscombs and a variety of intervening flowers, rosettes on two sides, and leaves on two sides. Two eagles are hidden in the crested swags, one in a blue and white print and the other in solid green on the opposite border.

This applique is a tribute to Indiana folk art. What a miracle that it has survived to appear in two publications seventy-five years apart—a real tribute to the excellent care it was given for the intervening years. In the 1915 photograph, deep creases showed which have now disappeared with proper care and storage.

Floral Sampler

Floral Sampler. Appliqued in twenty different blocks.
Made by the Great-great-grandmother McCasson of E. W. Ross. Terre Haute, Vigo County, Indiana.
Top circa 1850. Quilted 1910. Cotton. 89½" × 79". Collection of Vigo County Historical Society.

The Age of Elegance and Embroidery

5 Many Hoosiers looked back on the period beginning in the late 1800s and ending with the entrance of the U.S. into World War I as Indiana's golden age. Indiana writers such as James Whitcomb Riley, the "Hoosier Poet," and artists such as T. C. Steele were enjoying national renown. World-famous actors, musicians, and opera stars on tour performed at theaters even in not-so-big cities, while local groups of amateurs put on operettas and plays. Education and religion were thriving. The temperance movement, spearheaded by the Woman's Christian Temperance Union (WCTU), and the closely allied women's suffrage movement were gaining strength daily. While the railway system was still at its peak, automobiles (many of them manufactured in Indiana) were becoming more numerous as well, and roads were improving as a result. On May 11, 1911, the first Indianapolis 500-mile race was run. An excellent state park system was in the process of being created. As Indiana celebrated its statehood centennial in 1916, signs of prosperity and progress were everywhere.

A new woman was beginning to emerge at this time, one who was often college-educated and might aspire to a career in business, medicine, or teaching. She might even own and drive a car. At home, chores would be eased with the help of such electric appliances as irons, washing machines, and refrigerators.

In her leisure time the new woman enjoyed sports such as tennis, golf, and bicycling, and kept up with the latest novels. And she still enjoyed needlework, including quiltmaking.

Embroidered outline blocks featuring flowers, animals, or people were popular quilt motifs in the early twentieth century. Stamped blocks could be purchased at the dime store or ordered through various newspaper ads, or they could be hand drawn. Embroidery was done on the outlines, then the small blocks were assembled into a quilt. The usual color of the floss was either red or blue. Large numbers of these quilts were made especially for children, who previously had been treated like miniature adults. They did serve an educational purpose, as the different blocks taught them to recognize animals and flowers, as well as figures in history.

Newspaper ads for patterns flourished. Quilters could send for a new pattern or draft their own to size from the sketches that appeared in the newspaper. Contests sometimes developed from the blocks done in a particular series.

It was during this period that *The Ladies Home Journal* presented the Marie Webster quilts (see chapter 4). Her early designs showed an Art Nouveau influence, while the later ones were in Art Deco style. These patterns were a great departure from anything quiltmakers had attempted previously. The blocks were sometimes in a variety of sizes in

Ona Wilkinson.

Rosalie Wilkinson.

the same quilt, rather than being block repeats. All utilized unifying border designs and materials that were purchased especially for that project. No scrap quilts here!

Colors were softer, often pastels. Gone were the dark, somber colors of the Victorians. Quilt backgrounds and backing were most often white. The central medallion style returned, although the center might be achieved through the use of numerous smaller blocks.

The Wilkinson Art Quilt

(Hand-Made)

The Wilkinson Art Quilt owes its name and fame to the genius of Miss Ona Wilkinson of Ligonier, Indiana, and the close, vibrant cooperation of her sister Miss Rosalie Wilkinson, in whose artistic minds the quilt de luxe originated, whose smoldering ember of genius was fanned to a glowing flame by the gentle breeze of an ambition to give something better to the world.

Every Wilkinson Art Quilt made today is especially and individually designed by Miss Ona and Miss Rosalie and wrought by them with the assistance of a staff of devoted needle-workers; fashioned into that priceless something that embodies art and love above the scrupulous nicety of painstaking workmanship.

—From the catalog (Ligonier, Indiana: Wilkinson Quilt Company, n.d., but known to be pre-1926. Includes dated price list: 1915–1916)

Nellie Swartz (1903–   ).

The Misses Ona and Rosalie Wilkinson owned the Wilkinson Quilt Company in Ligonier, Noble County, Indiana. The sisters designed the Wilkinson Art Quilts and produced quilts for sale, with, as their catalog says, "the assistance of a staff of devoted needle-workers."

Quilts could be made to order; their 1916 catalog offered nine copyrighted selections of patterns and choices of cotton sateen, silk, and combinations of silk and sateen fabrics. Batting choices included cotton, wool, and down. According to the catalog, these were luxurious quilts "with all the charm of the old-fashioned sort, none of its lack of harmonious color and symmetrical design, and far out-rivaling it in warmth, lightness, and sanitary qualities." Even monograms—"a personal touch, aside from that found in the design"—could be added in a variety of styles.

For her first quilt, twenty-three-year-old Nellie Swartz purchased the fabric, pre-marked with chalk at the factory, along with wool batting, binding, and quilting thread, from the Wilkinson Quilt Company in the summer of 1926. The front side is blue, the back is a peach color. She quilted it herself, using blue thread. Nellie bought her quilt supplies just in time, because the Wilkinson Quilt Company burned to the ground later that year.

The Wilkinson Art Quilt

Diamond Scroll. Whole cloth quilt. Made by Nellie W. Swartz. Cromwell, Noble County, Indiana. 1926. Cotton sateen. 83" × 83". Designed by the Wilkinson sisters. Collection of the quiltmaker.

Swirl Quilt

Swirl. Pieced quilt. Maker and location unknown. Circa 1900. Cotton. 80½" × 69½".
Collection of Lynn Demaree.

This blue and cream swirl pattern rates as the most unusual pattern among the over 6,400 quilts registered by the IQRP. Owner Lynn Demaree doesn't know the quiltmaker, but believes the piece was made in Connecticut about 1890. The quilting is by hand, ten stitches to the inch, using the clamshell design, while the curved piecing of the quilt top itself was assembled mostly by machine.

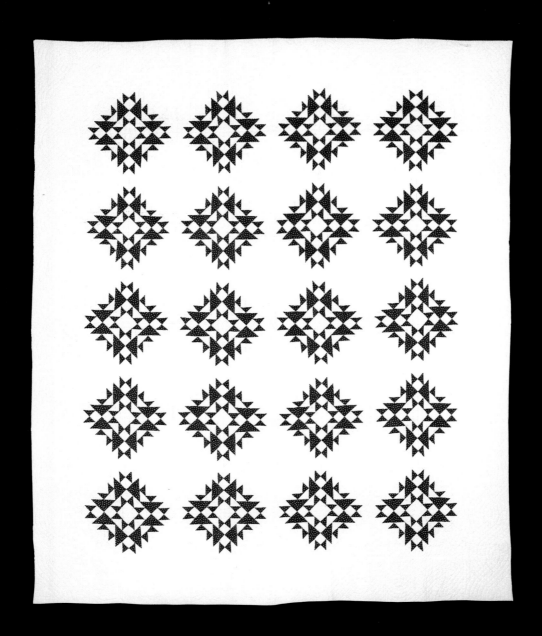

Crosses and Losses

Crosses and Losses. Family name is Double Stars. Pieced quilt. Made by Maria Schneider.
Quilted by Jennie Mae Foster Sullivan and her mother, Sarah Ann Rothenberger Foster.
Mulberry, Clinton County, Indiana. Circa 1890. Cotton. 88½" × 72½". Collection of Marilyn U. Lahr.

This crisp, geometric blue and white quilt was hand pieced by Maria Schneider in the early 1890s for her niece, Jennie Mae Foster Sullivan (1876–1962). Jennie and her mother, Sarah Ann Rothenberger Foster (1841–1921), hand quilted it. The quilt was made for Jennie's dowry. The family called the quilt pattern Double Stars, but it is known as Crosses and Losses in quilt pattern reference books.

The quilting is very fine and even, with twelve stitches to the inch. The quilters sewed cross-hatching in the pieced blocks, feathered wreaths in the plain blocks, and a cable through the borders.

A note was left with the quilt by Jennie's daughter, Mary Sullivan Burke, requesting that the quilt not be used for every day and stating that anyone who accepted it must take care of it. She wrote that she would rather the quilt leave the family than stay with someone who did not appreciate it.

Sarah Virginia Reynolds Oxley (1913–   ), wearing fashionable 1932 clothing and hairstyle.

The Indiana Puzzle contains three blocks, a dark square and a light square in alternating rows, and a patchwork block composed of squares and triangles that give the quilt motion. Set together, it takes off like an Indiana tornado!

Sarah Virginia Reynolds made her Indiana Puzzle quilt as part of her trousseau. Sarah was born in Delaware County in 1913 and married Charles M. Oxley in the parsonage of the Cowan Methodist Church in 1939. Her friend Leslie "Pete" Turner made the sandpaper template; his wife, Gladys, made a pink and white quilt from the same pattern.

The quilting was done by "Aunt" Cina Bowers, ninety-two, of Progress in 1932. Cina used three different quilting patterns for each of the three separate blocks that make up the crosspatch design. The white squares have a feathered wreath with a centered eight-point star and an eight-point star in each corner. The blue blocks have the same feathered wreath, but with cross-hatch centered and in the corners of the block. The pieced block has a flower design split into the four largest triangles and hanging diamonds on the center of the quilt. Each of the two borders has its own design. The blue border has a cable while the white has hanging diamonds. The heavy quilting boasts eleven stitches per inch. Sarah recalls that she pieced the three-block crosspatch pattern for the quilt on the machine.

The Indiana Puzzle

Indiana Puzzle. Pieced quilt. Made by Sarah Reynolds Oxley. Monroe Township, Delaware County, Indiana. Quilted by Cina Bowers of Progress. Circa 1931. Cotton. 91" × 76". Collection of the quiltmaker.

Sarah Gillibrand Bowers, shown in a photograph with her granddaughter, Hallie Hull Beatty, in 1923.

Sarah Gillibrand Bowers (1868–1943) was a loving and talented woman who brought up eleven children and still found time for needlework. At the time of her death, she had made ninety quilts for her children and grandchildren. Whenever possible she used their baby clothes in the quilts, and she stitched the initials of the intended recipient on each to prevent future squabbling.

Sarah loved flowers as much as she did quilting. To combine her two loves, she saved flower designs from baking soda boxes and used them as models for the flowers she stitched in her quilts. In this quilt, Sarah repeats ten large blocks with urns of red flowers with green leaves and stems in a two-way directional style. Between the large blocks Sarah placed ten smaller blocks containing her artistic flower patterns.

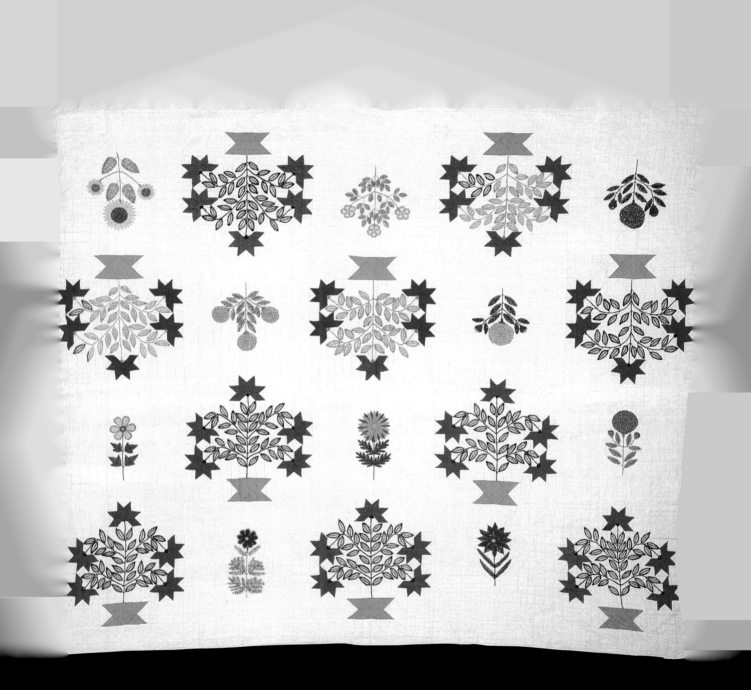

Sarah's Floral Sampler

Floral Sampler. Appliquéd, pieced, and embroidered quilt. Made by Sarah Gillibrand Bowers.
Greensburg, Decatur County, Indiana. Circa 1900. Cotton. 73" × 66½".
Collection of Elizabeth A. Beatty, great-granddaughter of the maker.

Fine needlework has been a traditional way for unmarried women to earn a living. Miss Cora Willis (1884–1976) and her sister Mary were the proprietors of a successful millinery shop on the town square in Boonville. When automobiles first came to this southern Indiana town, the sisters could afford to purchase an electric car and hire a young man to chauffeur them around. They took their meals at the St. Charles Hotel and were considered sophisticated businesswomen by the townspeople.

About 1920, Cora married George A. Roth, a widower with a young daughter. George was associated with the George J. Roth Department Store in Boonville, a quality dry goods establishment. He built a California bungalow at 401 Main Street for Cora as a wedding present. As was the custom, Cora left her business career and became a housewife and stepmother, but she did not abandon creativity. She designed and made many quilts, some of which were used as store decorations.

The basket is one-half of a Hole in the Barn Door pattern. Each is set on point in tan with red and green calico flowers. The plain blocks are beige and the quilt is surrounded with a border matching the flowers and blocks. It was made as a utility quilt, but it is beautiful nonetheless.

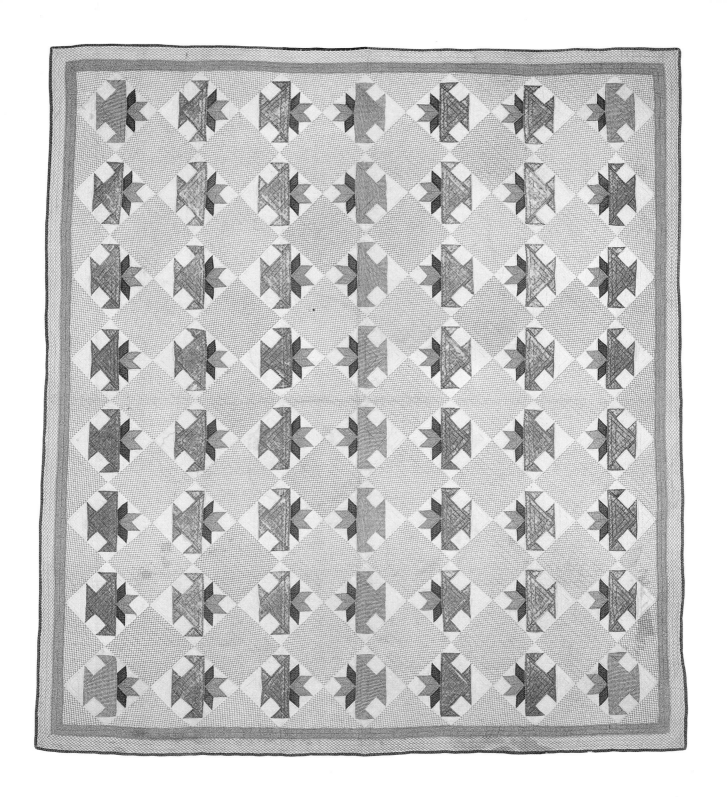

Barn Door Basket Quilt

*Basket. Pieced quilt. Made by Cora Willis Roth. Boonville, Warrick County, Indiana.
Circa 1925. Cotton. 80" × 71". Collection of Alice Hottenstein.*

Jennie Hesson.

Iva (left) and Golda Hesson.

This delightful quilt is one of a pair made by Jennie Hesson (1865–1946) for her daughters, Iva and Golda. Iva's quilt wore out long ago, but Golda's matching one remains, probably because she married late in life and had no children. Cottons used in the quilt include checks, plaids, plains, stripes, and florals, and the bright colors contrast with the light gray-green background. Buttonhole stitch embroidery outlines the children, and triple curved lines of quilting, nine stitches to the inch, meander through the blocks, sashing, and borders. Blocks such as these were available for purchase at local variety stores, but were usually outline-embroidered without the colorful fabric appliques. Imagine the joy of bedtime with these very special quilts!

Little People

Little People. Pattern also called Sunbonnet Girls and Boys.
Appliqued and embroidered quilt by Jennie Hesson. Summitville, Madison County, Indiana.
Circa 1920. Cotton. 78" × 68¾". Collection of Pamela Sue Smith.

Ruth Gertrude Jervis was just past her seventeenth birthday when she married Roy Farlow in September 1918.

Born in 1901 and still living, Ruth Farlow was a farmer's wife in the 1930s when she worked on her small stars quilt. It was scrap-pieced by hand from her dresses and those of her three daughters.

The colors follow concentric hexagons from the center, while two plain borders frame the quilt. The current owner, granddaughter Joan Manning, recalls, "Grandfather was mad at grandmother for spending so much time on this quilt."

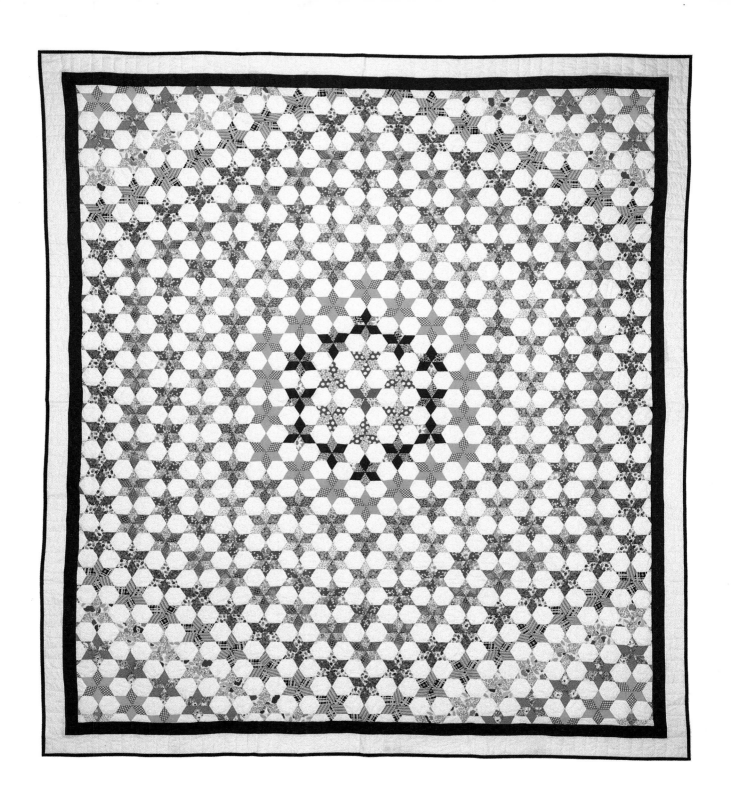

Concentric Star Rings

Star and Block. Family name, Six-Pointed Stars. Pieced quilt. Made by Ruth Gertrude Jervis Farlow.
Winchester, Randolph County, Indiana. Circa 1930. Quilted by Joan Manning. LaFountaine,
Wabash County, Indiana. Circa 1986. Cotton. 91½" × 82½". Collection of Joan Manning.

Mrs. Winslow's Puzzle

Solomon's Puzzle. Also known as Drunkard's Path. Pieced quilt. Maker Nettie Maude Johnson Winslow. Fairmount, Grant County, Indiana. Circa 1920. Cotton. 84¼" × 76". Collection of Julia Lewellen.

Nettie Maude Johnson Winslow.

Fairmount native Nettie Maude Johnson Winslow (1868–1943) made her Solomon's Puzzle quilt about 1920 from clothing scraps. According to her granddaughter Julia Lewellen, Nettie was a Quaker lady who married Jabez N. Winslow on 5 July 1885, had five children, and lived her entire life in Fairmount. The Winslow family in early Grant County was descended from a group who emigrated from England.

Starburst—The New York World's Fair Quilt

Starburst. Pieced quilt. Made by Lottie Ellen Merrill Owen (1896–1977).
Medaryville, Pulaski County, Indiana. Circa 1938–39. Cotton. 80" × 68". Collection of Nola J. Harper.

Lottie Ellen Merrill Owen (1896–1977) decided to make and enter her Starburst quilt in the 1939 New York World's Fair quilt display and contest.

In the hot yellow and oranges that had been selected by the fair committee, the pieced medallion center blends with the scalloped borders. The pieced sections are quilted in outlines and the plain areas have double feathers, stars, and diagonal lines. All Lottie's work was by hand. The quilt won an Honorable Mention at the World's Fair.

Originally from Clinton County, Lottie's family moved to the oil fields west of Medaryville at the turn of the century. She married Albert L. Owen in 1916 and had three children. To help with the expenses of a growing family, this quilt artist worked at the Medaryville Garment Factory until World War II when she was employed at the Kingsbury Ordnance Plant.

Clara Merriman in 1916.

With the quilting revival of the 1930s, it was a popular practice for newspapers to publish quilt patterns on their women's pages and sponsor contests based on them. Jointly sponsored by *The Marion Chronicle* and the Marion Public Library, one such contest was climaxed with a three-day exhibit, May 21–23, 1930, at the library where the winning quilts were on display and prizes were awarded.

Judges for the contest were Marie Daugherty Webster, author of *Quilts, Their Story and How to Make Them*; Mrs. Lora Lillard, who with her partner Mrs. Hiram Beshore operated the Practical Patchwork Company, a mail order business in stamped quilts which used the designs of Mrs. Webster; and Miss Eva Stanton, an artist and designer affiliated with Marion's very exclusive Vogue Shop, who had won a scholarship to study art at the John Herron Art Institute in Indianapolis.

The five-dollar first prize was won by Mrs. Clara Woods for her expertise in "embroidery, good quilting, accuracy in joining, neatness." Her quilt depicted a Sunbonnet Girl and Boy entering a garden through a gate in the white picket fence border. The garden is composed of alternating green blocks and embroidered flowers, patterns for which had been published in the newspaper.

Clara Merriman Woods (1887–1976) was born in Porter County, Indiana, and married Edward Woods in 1923. They had no children. Clara worked as a sales clerk at Blumenthal's Department Store, but needlework was her passion. She taught classes in various forms of needle arts.

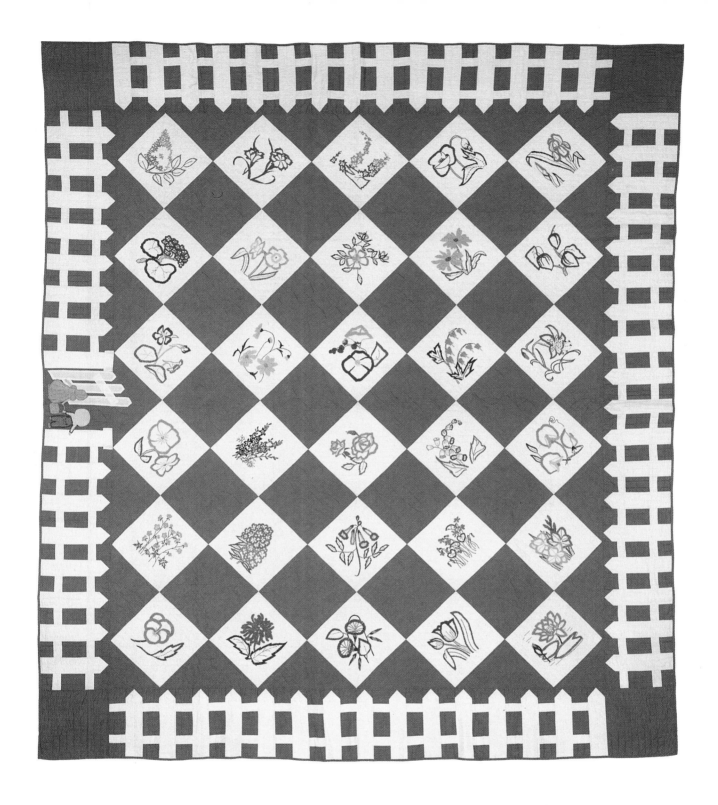

The Flower Garden Quilt Contest

Flower Garden. Embroidered quilt. Made by Clara Merriman Woods. Marion, Grant County, Indiana. Circa 1930. 89" × 76". Cotton. Collection of Margaret Merriman Moore.

Lonnie Elsie Medsker Dixon. Renowned for her flower gardens, she is shown among her dahlias.

The *Indianapolis Star* has been the most prolific quilt contest sponsor in the state. One of its early contests featured this Nancy Page Quilt Club pattern series called Garden Bouquet. Birds named Saucy and Sassy appear on each block, while each urn holds a flower of a different variety. Series quilts, popular in the 1930s, contained twelve or more different patterns that were published at regular intervals in newspapers of the day. Meant to be set with plain blocks, the series was thus enough for a quilt. Series with both adult and juvenile themes were available. During contests sponsored by newspapers, a different pattern was published each week; more blocks sold more newspapers.

Lonnie Elsie Medsker Dixon (1875–1971) of Martinsville entered her Bluebirds quilt in this contest. The twenty pieced and appliqued blocks are set on point with twelve plain blocks. Each block is finished with embroidery, and the quilting is thirteen stitches to the inch. Her quilt won an Honorable Mention.

Lonnie quilted for hire, charging one cent per yard of thread. She also crocheted, tatted, and made tiny fishnets for handling the goldfish that were raised at the Grassyforks Fish Hatcheries. During World War I she made bandages for wounded soldiers.

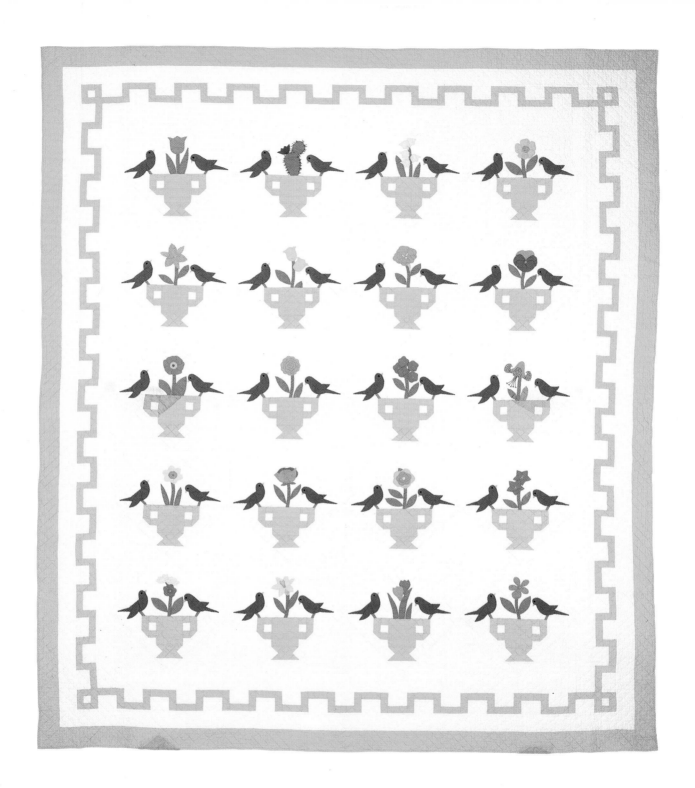

The Indianapolis Star Quilt Contest

Bluebirds. Also called Garden Bouquet. Pieced and appliqued quilt. Made by Lonnie Elsie Medsker Dixon. Martinsville, Morgan County, Indiana. Circa 1930. Cotton. 99" × 84". Collection of Nina M. Canatsey.

The Gray-Green Depression Era

6 By 1920 the modern Indiana woman had the vote, Prohibition was in effect, the population of Indiana was just under three million, and the census showed that for the first time there were more urban Hoosiers than rural ones. Younger people especially were moving to town in search of a better life. There was concern among the older generation about the evil influence of motion pictures, radio, and new styles of popular music and dance—and especially the freedom afforded by the automobile. The new woman shortened her skirts, cut her hair, and perhaps even took up smoking.

The rural-to-urban trend was set back somewhat by the onset of the Depression, when many city dwellers lost their jobs and returned to the farm. Another effect of the Depression was a decline in railways. It seemed nothing could stop the rise of the automobile, however; cars had become so numerous that in 1929 having a driver's licence became state law.

During the Depression, thousands were unemployed in Indiana. Many Hoosier couples postponed marriage or practiced family planning until such time as prosperity returned. The population increased only 5.8 percent from 1930 to 1940, to just under three and a half million. This decade also saw the coming to power of Indiana Democrats and the advent of President Franklin Delano Roosevelt's New Deal. It also saw the last of Prohibition; although it had been enthusiastically supported by the Woman's Christian Temperance Union and the major Protestant churches, the "noble experiment" came to an end in 1933. However, the state continued to prohibit Sunday sales, and various licensing requirements were strictly enforced. New state and federal welfare programs were set up to help the unemployed and the aged, and a state income tax was put into effect.

Also during those years Indiana quilters elevated the scrap quilt to an art form. The most popular patterns in pieced quilts—Grandmother's Flower Garden, Double Wedding Ring, and Dresden Plate—were all scrap-type quilts.

Grandmother's Flower Garden is a hexagon mosaic quilt. Although the basic design is very old, the use and arrangement of colors to signify the flowers and paths or grass in the flower bed is tied to the Depression era. A special shade of green with a muted gray tone is generally recognized as the prevailing color of 1930s quilts. It was frequently combined with pink, lavender, or yellow, in pastel hues. Scraps of various muslin prints were combined to form the flowers. Of the quilts registered from this era, the majority were Grandmother's Flower Gardens. It was not an easy pattern to execute because the template has six equal sides and the top had to be pieced entirely by hand.

The second most popular pattern was the Dresden Plate, formed of a circle of petals with a large center. Each petal was a scrap of fabric; these could be arranged in a ring of random or repeat colors to form the flower. The petals could end with a rounded end or a pointed end, or the two shapes could be alternated in some manner. The Dresden Plate is first pieced, by hand or machine, and then appliqued onto a block of solid color muslin. The background color most often used was white.

Double Wedding Ring pattern quilts did exist in the nineteenth century and some of these were registered with IQRP, but the majority come from the Depression era or later. With its large interlocking rings or circles, the Double Wedding Ring is easily recognized by non-quilters. The intersections of the circles were handled in a variety of ways by different quilters. Some used two colors for the four-patch block that made up the intersection. Others used one color for the four-patch and surrounded it with green pieces which gave the effect of leaves. This was another pattern that was not easy to execute accurately.

In the Depression's early years favored colors were pastels, but from about 1939 onward the colors brightened and became bolder. World War II naturally inspired a revival of red, white, and blue combinations.

Although quiltmakers had been purchasing dime store blocks and patterns for decades and quilt kits too had been available, kits were used in especially great numbers during the Depression. Many of these kit quilts were elegantly designed using quality fabrics; when made up by a skilled craftsworker an heirloom could result.

Arrena Price Smith with her granddaughter Anne, who is wearing a
dress Arrena wore as a child.

When Arrena Price Smith (1857–1948) and her daughter Lodie Smith Stallsmith began this pastel quilt, they intended it for four-year-old Anne, Arrena's granddaughter. They used scraps from some of Anne's clothes and taught her how to piece and sew so that she could add a few stitches to the quilt. When Anne was married in 1948, the quilt was her grandmother's wedding gift to her. Arrena died that same year.

The Double Wedding Ring blocks are set into the quilt and surrounded with a wide peach border edged with Prairie Points.

Arrena, called Rena by friends, was raised as a Quaker in rural Franklin Township, Grant County, Indiana. She attended the Deer Creek Monthly Meeting of Friends, and taught school until her marriage to Robert L. Smith, of a Quaker family from Mississinewa Monthly Meeting. They lived near Marion with their two daughters, Irma and Lodie.

Rena was one of the earliest members of the Deer Creek Woman's Christian Temperance Union (WCTU). For seventeen years she served as secretary of the county organization. One WCTU project was organizing speech contests for young people, with medals awarded to winning contestants. Concerned that nearly all the contestants were girls, Mrs. Smith persuaded a group of boys to participate. According to L. O. Chasey, one of the "gang," all the boys under Mrs. Smith's tutelage went on to become successful citizens—a tribute to her influence.

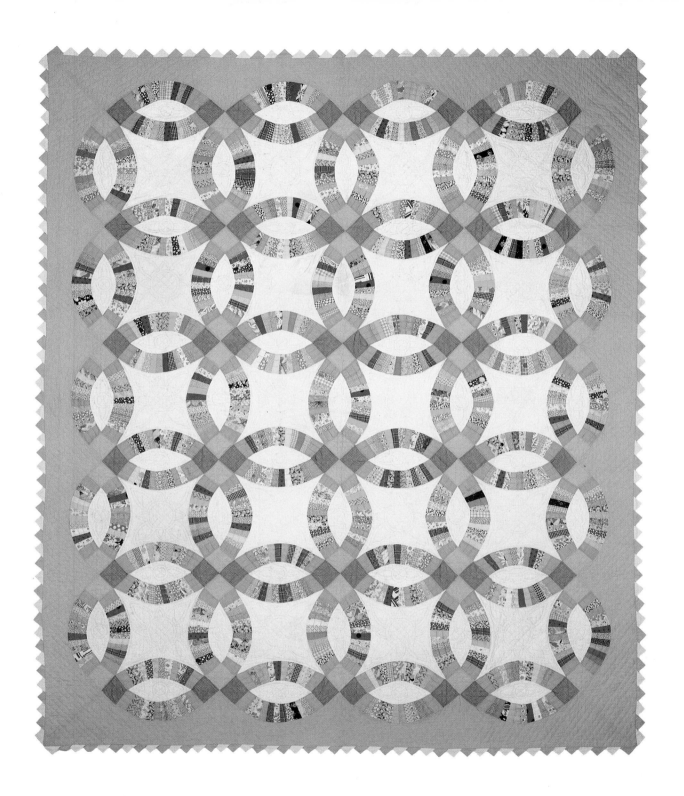

Anne's Double Wedding Ring

Double Wedding Ring. Pieced quilt. Made by Arrena Price Smith. Marion, Grant County, Indiana. 1932. Cotton. 104½" × 87½". Collection of Anne Werry, granddaughter of the maker.

Grandmother's Flower Garden with Leaves

Grandmother's Flower Garden with Leaves. Pieced quilt. Maker and origin unknown. Circa 1930.
Cotton. 78" × 69½". Collection of Kay Carroll.

Quilts made from hexagon shapes were extremely popular during the 1930s. The Grandmother's Flower Garden with Leaves pattern is from this era. This quilt boasts a wonderful array of scraps which compose the flowers. The "garden" is bordered with plain bright yellow hexagons and green hexagons are used as leaves. The quiltmaker is unknown, but her bright and cheerful quilt is like a ray of sunshine.

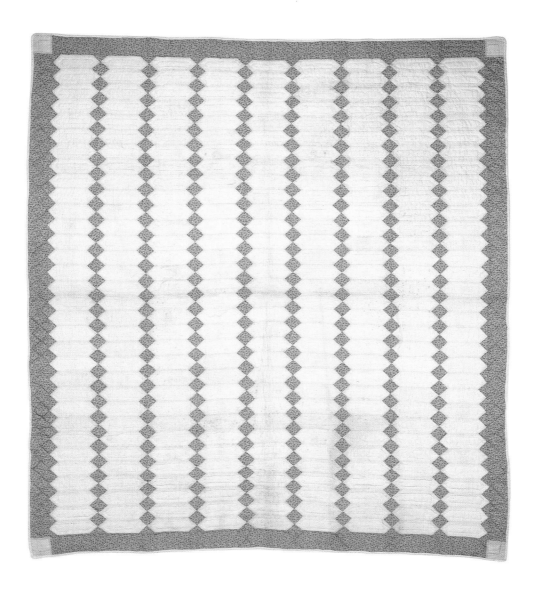

From Tobacco Sacks to Church Windows

Church Windows. Pieced quilt by Mary Ruth Vernon Iden. Wabash, Wabash County, Indiana. 1935. Quilted by Maude (Mrs. Verlin) Mullett in 1983. Cotton. 81" × 76". Collection of Robert Iden.

According to Robert Iden, the owner of this quilt, in the 1930s loose tobacco for "roll-your-own" cigarettes came in small muslin sacks tied with a yellow drawstring, affixed to which was a fancy label that "was always hung outside the pocket." The cigarette papers were attached to the outside of the bag. Brand names included Bull Durham, Duke's Mixture, and Golden Grain, to name a few. All this for only five cents!

Mr. Iden recalls that he and his younger brother, Darrell, "picked up" many of the empty bags that his seventy-three-year-old Grandmother Iden (1862–1936) ripped apart for quilt pieces, adding scraps left over from their mother's new dress. Combining the unbleached muslin and the pink floral print, Mary Ruth pieced this Church Windows quilt as a tenth birthday gift for Darrell in 1935. She died before it was finished. Darrell kept the top until his own death nearly fifty years later.

While attending the widow's sale in 1982, Robert spotted the quilt top and bought it for sixty dollars. He then paid Mrs. Mullett one hundred dollars to quilt it for him. Now the quilt brings back many happy memories of a boyhood Darrell and Robert shared together.

Lela Duckwall Vore.

Lela Duckwall Vore (1896–1980), born in Howard County, Indiana, moved to a farm in Delaware County after her marriage to George Vore. As a farmer's wife with two children she led a hard and hectic life. She lived without a telephone or electricity and made many utilitarian quilts of necessity.

Facing the bleak Depression years, Lela started her masterpiece quilt. Her close friend Fannie Carmin, a dressmaker, helped Lela plan the colors. Over the next ten years the quilt was continued little by little. Once when she picked it up she was dismayed to find that it had to be mended because a mouse had chewed holes in it. This was to be Lela's only appliqued quilt.

Primrose and Grapes is an unusual design for the Depression era. It was based on Bouquet of Garden Flowers, a quilt made by Emma Ann Covert of Lebanon, Ohio, in 1842, that is pictured in *The Romance of the Patchwork Quilt in America* by Carrie Hall and Rose Kretsinger (1935). The nine-block setting in the center was a style used in mid-nineteenth century quilts. The quilt could be placed four ways on the bed and still appear correct. It is finished with two shorter borders of flower urns and two longer urn and flower borders.

Although Lela used a nineteenth-century design, her fabrics are in typical Depression-era colors. The same pinks, lavenders, greens, and golds are seen repeated in countless Grandmother's Flower Gardens, Double Wedding Rings, and Dresden Plate quilts of the period.

Primrose and Grapes Quilt

Primrose and Grapes. Appliqued quilt by Lela Duckwall Vore. Gaston-Eaton area, Delaware County, Indiana. Circa 1927–37. Cotton. 82″ × 80″. Collection of Mrs. Mary E. Jones, daughter of the maker.

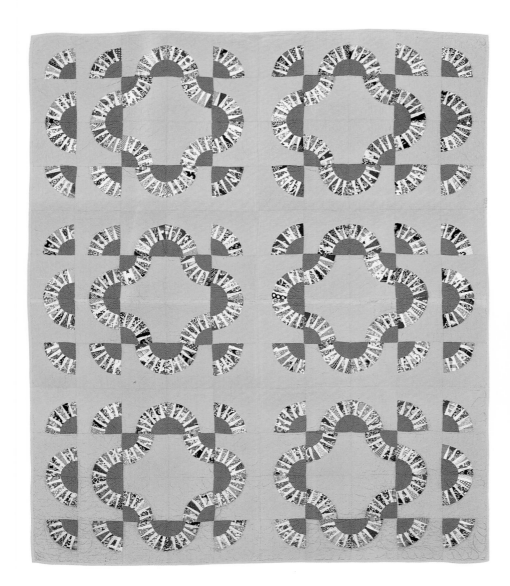

Naomi Shields aged twelve, a year before she made the Japanese Fans quilt.

Japanese Fans

Japanese Fans. Also called Mohawk Trail. Pieced quilt. Made by Naomi Shields Stillions. Bloomington, Monroe County, Indiana. 1929. Cotton. 79½" × 65½". Collection of the maker.

Naomi Shields grew up on a farm south of Bloomington. With four younger children to look after, her busy mother put Naomi to work sewing and mending when she was only ten. At the age of thirteen, she made this bright fan quilt. The contents of her scrap bag had proved insufficient, so she traded two hens to the owner of the local general store to obtain the yellow and lavender fabrics she needed. From the smaller pieced fan blocks, Naomi built six sets of larger fan formations. Two pieced borders of fans complete the quilt.

In 1940 Naomi Shields married Osborne Stillions (1913–1988), who spent the next five years overseas with the Army Corps of Engineers and later worked for Otis Elevator. They were the parents of a daughter, Kiva Stillions Branam (b. 1950). Naomi worked at RCA in Bloomington for thirty-seven years, then at several local fabric stores. In 1975 she opened her own fabric store in Bloomington, which specializes in quilters' supplies. She still makes several quilts a year and also enjoys many other forms of needlework.

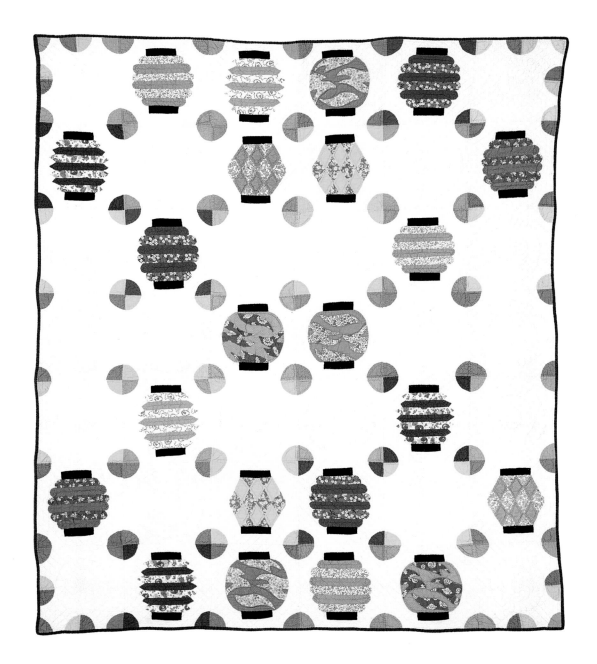

Chinese Lanterns

Chinese Lanterns. Appliqued quilt. Made by Etta Mae Clark Summitt. Vernon, Jennings County, Indiana. 1935–45. Cotton. 74" × 63". Collection of Mary Summitt Galliher.

Etta Mae Clark Summitt's Chinese Lanterns quilt shows unusual design and colors. Each of the twenty-two lanterns is uniquely appliqued. Feathered wreaths are hidden in the quilting of the plain white blocks, while the appliqued blocks have extra quarter circles appliqued into the corners, forming multicolored balls at the block intersections.

Etta (1901–1974) worked at the Ward Stilson Clothing Factory in Anderson, making house dresses and ceremonial uniforms for fraternal lodges. She also did all kinds of home sewing, from clothing to home furnishings. She belonged to the Meadowbrook Baptist Church and the Toll Gate Homemakers Club.

Treva Seidner Main and Adrian
Main of Muncie, Bearcat fans and
quiltmakers, in 1940.

Indiana's obsession with basketball inspired this husband-and-wife team effort. In 1932 Adrian Main designed and cut the pieces for a medallion-style commemorative quilt honoring Muncie Central High School's formidable Bearcats. Predictably, he used the team colors—royal purple and white. His wife, Treva, did the piecing, appliqueing, and quilting. Large basketballs are used for the quilting motifs on the center section of the quilt.

Treva Maude Seidner was born in Randolph County in 1899 and married Adrian Main there in 1918. Besides caring for her family Treva worked full time at the Warner Gear Transmission Plant in Muncie. Their daughter, Thelma Main Brown, now owns the quilt.

The Muncie Bearcats have captured the Indiana State Championship in boys' basketball a total of eight times in this century. The names embroidered on the quilt are, on left side, the 1928 team: Charles Secrist, center; Hays Young, guard; Robert Yohler, forward; Robert Parr, forward; Ralph Satterlee, forward; Eugene Eber, guard; Francis Reed, guard; Carleton Walsh, forward; Carl Cheek, forward, and Glenn Wolfe, forward. In the center is "Coach Jolley"; on the right side, the 1931 team: Jack Mann, center; Lauren Lowery, center; Robert Schuck, forward; Charles Davison, forward; Eugene Curtis, back guard; Cleon Cook, forward; Glyn Rivers, floor guard; Charles Icerman, floor guard; and Eugene Smith, forward. The Indiana Basketball Hall of Fame opened in 1990 and has four major exhibits, one of which is dedicated to the Bearcats. The other three honor Crawfordsville as the cradle of Indiana basketball, Indianapolis's Crispus Attucks for its contribution as a black high school, and Milan for the most famous of all state championship games, the one with the Bearcats which inspired the movie *Hoosiers*.

State Basket Ball Champions 1928

The Bearcat Quilt

Bearcat Quilt. Pieced and appliqued by Treva Maude Seidner Main. Muncie, Delaware County, Indiana. 1932. Cotton. 81½" × 69". Collection of Thelma Brown.

Eva Anthony DePue.

This graceful 1930s Iris quilt was the first quilt registered by the IQRP during the first registry day, April 11, 1987, at Vincennes.

Eva Anthony DePue (1901–1949) stitched her Irises from lavender, purple, and green cotton sateen and framed them with a wonderful watermelon-style border using scallops, points, and oval corners. Set on point rather than horizontal and vertical, the twelve appliqued Iris blocks are quilted with hanging diamonds, while each of the six solid color lavender blocks contains a fleur-de-lis. Matching fleur-de-lis designs are quilted into the points on the edges of the border. Embroidery has been added to the flowers. The quilting thread is pink and flannel sheeting was used as filler. To make the binding, the top and backing were each folded into the middle and stitched together.

Eva's Irises

Iris. Appliqued quilt. Made by Eva Anthony DePue. Location unknown, probably Iowa. Circa 1930.
Cotton sateen. 101¼" × 78½". Collection of Evelyn DePue McClure.

Mary Ward Calhoun.

This Cactus Basket is a colorful quilt of forty-two pieced blocks set on point and alternating with plain blocks. It was made in 1941 by Mary Ward Calhoun (1865–1949), of Atlanta in Hamilton County. Mary purchased her fabrics at Essig's Grocery Store and made the quilt as a gift to her granddaughter.

The one-way directional set of the blocks is enhanced by the elegant swag borders, reminiscent of a nineteenth century quilt, but the green, purple, and pink colors are definitely 1930s-40s. The pieced blocks are outline quilted, while the plain blocks have feathered wreath quilting. The border is quilted on the diagonal. The quilt is bound with rounded corners and scalloped edges.

Cactus Basket

Cactus Basket. Pieced quilt. Made by Mary Ward Calhoun. Atlanta, Hamilton County, Indiana. 1941.
Cotton. 85½" × 72". Collection of Mary M. Clemans.

Amandana Stewart Pribble.

Helen Uebele Lohrig.

Amandana Pribble chose an unusual setting for her fan quilt in the pattern commonly called Gypsy Trail or Snake in the Hollow. Although a scrap quilt, the blue calico patches give it continuity and direction. As was popular in the 1950s, Helen Lohrig used commercial binding on the edges.

Amandana Stewart Pribble (1885–1941) grew up in Vineyard, Switzerland County, Indiana. Her paternal great-grandfather had settled on 160 acres in Switzerland County in 1798. Her father was the postmaster and Craig Township Trustee. Amandana,

named for her grandmother, married Henry Pribble.

Widowed at forty-seven, Helen Uebele Lohrig (1885–1970) became head cook for the Inn at Clifty Falls State Park in Madison, Indiana. She lived in a cottage on the park grounds, where she liked to quilt in her spare time.

The only child of Amandana and Henry Pribble, a daughter, married Helen Lohrig's son. Amandana died before she could quilt her top, so Helen finished Amandana's Gypsy Trail for the granddaughter they shared, who is its present owner.

Amandana's Gypsy Trail

Gypsy Trail or Snake in the Hollow. Pieced quilt. Top by Amandana Stewart Pribble. Vineyard, Switzerland County, Indiana. Circa 1930. Quilted by Helen Uebele Lohrig. Madison, Jefferson County, Indiana. Circa 1950. Cotton. 87¾" × 67½". Collection of Mary Ann Plummer.

Lillie Mae Terwilliger Castor.

Lillie Mae Terwilliger Castor (1894–1973) began the quilt, Down the Garden Path, in 1945 and finished it in 1955 for her granddaughter, Lucretia Su Lawler. Lucretia related that Lillie married Franklin Harrison Castor in 1915 and they farmed in Tipton County until the Depression, when they lost the farm. The Castors moved with their four children to become tenant farmers on the Forkner Farm north of Anderson. Frank died in 1944. Lillie became one of four widows who quilted together. The other three were Gert Cooper, Loy Paddock, and Lottie Blacklidge. They all lived at the intersection of State Road 128 and Madison Avenue in Madison County.

Lillie's quilting frame was in her sunroom on the east side of the house and was active most of the year. Each of Lillie's thirteen grandchildren was allowed to choose a quilt top from her blanket chest and she completed it as a wedding gift. Lucretia, however, asked for hers as a college graduation gift, because she wasn't thinking of getting married.

A prolific quilter, Lillie sold two or three quilts every year, and at the time of her death in 1973, after fulfilling all promises made to her grandchildren, still had several pieced tops in the blanket chest.

This striking quilt is red and white with multicolored scraps forming the fans in each block. The backing is red cotton. Framing the top is an ice cream cone–style border of red and white. Other names for this pattern are Railroad around Rocky Mountain and Snake Trail.

Down the Garden Path

Down the Garden Path. Pieced quilt. Made by Lillie Mae Terwilliger Castor.
Anderson, Madison County, Indiana. 1945–1955. Cotton. 85" × 78". Collection of Lucretia Su Lawler.

Opal Marie Bevington, who made the Tulip quilt from the captured Nazi flag.

Pvt. Forest Bevington in early 1942, Camp Claiborne, Louisiana, shown with his Browning Automatic Rifle, which he called "a tough gun to master."

Following their marriage in 1912, Opal and Jesse Bevington had one son and one daughter. When her son returned safely from World War II with a captured enemy flag, Opal cut it into tulips to make this quilt. (The red German flag with its familiar black and white swastika was a big 12′ × 12′ in size.)

Forest relates: "I was a school teacher when I was ordered to report for a physical and induction into the U.S. Army in July 1941. Being twenty eight, I was too old, and returned to teaching, but after the attack on Pearl Harbor I was no longer too old, and was snatched from my classroom. I soon ended up in Co. C, 82nd Div., U.S. Army Infantry, Camp Claiborne, Louisiana. After my training there, I was transferred to Co. D (Heavy Weapons), 44th Infantry Division, and sent to Europe. In the spring of 1945 I was in Austria, a first lieutenant, we had many casualties and many promotions, and the flag was taken from a flagpole at Brenner Pass in the Austrian Alps. After Germany surrendered [in May] our company was ordered to the Pacific, but the Japanese surrender [in August] brought us back home.

"My Mother was always busy with some kind of needlework and she used the German flag for a quilt."

Tulips

Tulips. Appliqued and embroidered quilt made by Opal Marie Ray Bevington. Fort Wayne, Allen County, Indiana. 1946–1950. Cotton. 110" × 95". Collection of Forest and Betty Bevington.

Oriental Splendor

Oriental Splendor. Pieced quilt. Made by Alice D. Iler. Elwood, Madison County, Indiana. 1927. Cotton. 93" × 78". Collection of Marian Hart.

This Oriental Splendor quilt was called Red and White Stars by the family of Alice D. Iler when she finished it in 1927 as a gift for her niece Marian Hart.

Marian remembers that Alice was born in Tipton County and graduated from Anderson Business College. Her first and only job was for a Mr. Macelgrave of Elwood who owned a box company. Alice was once engaged, but her fiancé drowned. She enjoyed card playing and golf, but in her later years travel was her greatest love. She disliked cooking and housework and ate every meal out.

Oriental Splendor has 214 triangle-shaped blocks and the sashing is constructed to show LeMoyne Stars where the blocks join. The triangular shape is continued to form an unusual diamond edge for the quilt on two sides.

Indiana, Crossroads of America

7 During World War II, while the men went off to war, women replaced men on factory assembly lines, in Indiana as in the rest of the country. After the war women were expected to return to the home, and did so in great numbers. Domesticity and the family reigned supreme. *McCall's Magazine* styled it the era of "Togetherness." In the 1960s they gradually began to reenter the work force, but now sought to combine jobs with caring for homes and families.

For those who could still find enough hours in the day for needlework, quilts continued to be made for gifts, special events, celebrations, and commemoratives.

The prevailing colors in the 1950s were pale pink or blue with gray or black, and the Log Cabin pattern enjoyed a revival. Colors progressed to orange, teal, brown, lime green, and avocado or dark green in the 1960s and 1970s. The Bicentennial saw a surge of quiltmaking as women endeavored to leave their mark. Star patterns again were popular as a way to symbolize this celebration. Neon colors electrified the 1980s.

More kits were sold. Classes were started and fabric stores especially designed to serve quilters were developed. Magazines were published to bring the quilter the latest in patterns and notions.

By the 1970s the quilt began to be considered as an art form, rather than just a craft. National and international exhibits, conventions, seminars, and symposiums were organized and devoted to promoting quiltwork.

Quilts were elevated from the bed to the wall. Wall quilts registered with the project were almost exclusively from the last twenty years. Their dimensions were no longer dictated by the size of a bed.

Perhaps most importantly, the success of quilt history projects documenting quilts, quiltmakers, and the history they embody has caused America to reconsider the quilt and the rightful place of its maker as a part of our heritage.

It is interesting to speculate in just what ways the quilts of the future will continue to evolve, since quiltmaking to some extent always reflects the times, location, and circumstances in which it takes place.

R. Emma Abroham with her grand-daughter, Mary Ellen Dewey, in 1961.

With the implementation of the interstate highway program, Indiana gained a number of important highways. Twelve interstates crisscross the state; four plus U.S. 40, the National Road, converge on the Circle City of Indianapolis, while I-465 rings its perimeter. With more miles of interstate than any other state its size in the nation, it has adopted the motto, "Indiana, Crossroads of America."

In 1952, South Bend native R. Emma Kovach Abroham designed and pieced her quilt in red, white, and blue—the colors of the interstate road markers. On it she put the state's new motto and the state flower at that time, the Zinnia. She bought the fabrics at Wyman's Department Store and later gave the quilt to her daughter, Alice Dewey.

Emma saw her first quilt, a wool Log Cabin, as a twelve-year-old while shopping at Brugner's Drug Store at Main and Jefferson in South Bend, and was impressed. She made her first quilt of simple squares when she was seventeen.

Born in 1908, Emma is a prolific quiltmaker who has designed many wonderful, whimsical, and unusual quilts. Some of her graphs and drawings have appeared in *McCall's Needlework Magazine.* Her father encouraged her creativity: Always be original, he told her, and never copy the work of others. These words have become her personal motto.

"Indiana, Crossroads of America"

Pieced quilt by R. Emma Abroham. South Bend, St. Joseph County, Indiana. 1952. Cotton. 96" × 83". Collection of Alice Abroham Dewey.

Alerting children to traffic dangers was the goal of the two women who inspired the 1986 quilt "Saved by the Belt." Jennifer Stephanidis and Dr. Karen Stroup were working with Automotive Safety for Children at James Whitcomb Riley Hospital for Children in Indianapolis. They shared their ideas with the Indiana Association of Women Highway Safety Leaders, Inc., who joined in enthusiastically, and the Quilters' Guild of Indianapolis, who agreed to make the quilt.

The quilt shows an outline of the state and some of its famous landmarks, with roads connecting the various places. Carol Clemons of QGI researched and designed the quilt. She drew the landmarks, made silkscreens, and printed them onto cotton fabrics. Other guild members helped with the applique and the quilting.

The background is pieced squares on which the Embroiderers' Guild stitched the names of children under four years of age who survived vehicle accidents because they were wearing seat belts. The border resembles a seat belt and encircles the quilt, buckling at the top or northern border of the state.

The quilt has traveled throughout Indiana to schools and libraries to give children the message. A teaching packet accompanies it. Ms. Pat Nowak, a fourth grade teacher at the Oaklandon Elementary School, said, "The quilt had a dual purpose here. We used it because it goes right along with our Indiana history studies, but all along we did exercises that made the students think about safety and seat belts."

Saved by the Belt

Appliqued and pieced quilt. Designed by Carol Clemons. Constructed by the Quilters' Guild of Indianapolis. Embroidered by the Embroiderers' Guild. Indianapolis, Marion County, Indiana. 1986. 90" × 65". Collection of the Indiana Association of Highway Safety Leaders, Inc.

William Kent Watson poses with a prize-winning photograph from his Speedway collection. The photo shows A. J. Foyt and his car.

William Kent Watson has been an Indianapolis Motor Speedway staff photographer for twenty-five years. Each year he spends every May weekend at the track. His wife, Ruth Ann Raver Watson, designed, pieced, tied, and quilted this medallion quilt for him.

Ruth Ann used the embroidered panel from Bill's first uniform shirt back as the center block and built a checkered flag framework around it. At the foot of the quilt are blocks based on the various signal flags used in U.S. auto racing. She used cotton and synthetic materials for the top, batt, and backing. Since she used a thick batt, Ruth Ann both quilted and tied it together.

Begun in 1911, the Indianpolis 500 is the nation's oldest continuing auto race. It has the largest one-day attendance of any sporting event in the world and draws fans worldwide.

INDIANAPOLIS
MOTOR SPEEDWAY
Staff
Photographer
Bill Watson

The 500 Mile Race Quilt

Indy 500 Race. Pieced medallion style quilt. Made by Ruth Ann Raver Watson. Muncie, Delaware County, Indiana. 1987. Cotton-polyester. 84″ × 58″. Collection of William Kent Watson.

In August 1987, Indiana and the City of Indianapolis hosted the Pan Am Games, a prestigious event held every four years in the summer preceding the Olympic Games year.

Hoosiers have a long-standing reputation for being avid sports fans and for staging first-class athletic events. For the Tenth Pan Am Games, the city and state offered modern facilities, an army of volunteers, and plenty of enthusiasm. Over 30,000 volunteers from throughout the state spent countless hours preparing and staging the games, during which more than 4,000 athletes from thirty-seven Western Hemisphere nations participated in thirty sports.

Quilts have often been made to commemorate important events, and members of Quilters Too, a special interest group of the Marion County Extension Homemakers, decided to preserve their memories of the Tenth Pan Am Games through a quilt.

Before beginning, the group had to obtain authorization, specific instructions, and approval for use of the logo, official mascot, "Amigo," and sports pictograms from Pan Am Games officials. The volunteers were required to use only black and white for the thirty pictograms, and only the official Pan Am colors for the mascot and logo. Constructing this quilt were: Virginia Barnes, Delores Bowling, Patricia Boyles, Josephine Cox, Emalou Garten, Alice Higdon, Jean Hollenbaugh, Harriett Kennon, Mary La Rose, Esther Link, Joan Matthews, Rita Marie Rosner, Vida Smith, Eleanor Sowder, Shirley Stumpf, and Pauline Ward.

The Pan Am Games Quilt

Tenth Pan Am Games. Applique quilt. Made by Quilters Too of the Marion County Extension Homemakers.
Marion County, Indiana, 1986. Cotton, 67¾" × 65¾". Collection of the Indiana Sports Corporation.

Muncie's High Street Methodist Church suffered a disaster in the bitter winter of 1978 when a gas explosion destroyed the building. But the members pulled together, and in time the building was rebuilt. To celebrate the 150th anniversary of the church in 1986 and the joy of having survived the tragedy with no loss of life, eight women were selected to construct a commemorative quilt.

The quilt has nine appliqued blocks surrounded by sixteen plain blocks. The circles represent unending love, the quatrefoils, the four gospels. The center block design with a cross and crown is from the top of their chancel window. The cross and the flame symbolize the United Methodist Church. In the second row center block is a sketch of their first church, at the corner of Elm and Washington Streets. The lower right hand appliqued block depicts the welcome doors of the church. Other blocks symbolize friendship and the sacraments.

The committee consisted of Joyce Kaufman, chairperson; Judy Luzadder, artist and coordinator; Ginny Demaree and Gerry Harris, (both now deceased), Marty Raisor, Marilyn Williams, Paula Faunce, and Jan Sturgeon.

A rich burgundy shade was chosen for the circles, quatrefoils, border, sashing, and binding, while a cream color was used for the background. The wedding block, done by Paula Faunce, shows the bride in her white satin gown complete with ruffle. Under her veil is her curly blonde hair. Beads were used as buttons down the back of the gown.

Church Commemorative

Church Commemorative. Appliqued and pieced. Women's Committee of the High Street Methodist Church. Muncie, Delaware County, Indiana. 1986. Cotton. 74" × 73¾". Collection of High Street Methodist Church.

"To promote equity and opportunity for women" is the slogan of the Fort Wayne Women's Bureau, formed in 1976 to help women in need. In celebration of ten years of service, Alison R. Adams of Fort Wayne designed an original quilt.

The five large blocks are symbolic. The center block of the quilt shows women from various walks of life, reaching out to all the others. The lower left block shows women's influence in the arts, music, and literature. The traditional roles of wife, mother, and homemaker are depicted in the upper left block. Women reaching into medicine and the sciences are in the upper right block, while service occupations held by women are in the lower right of these five blocks.

Four smaller squares surround the center block. They show the symbols of a woman's right to vote: a sheaf of wheat and a rose. The four gold rectangles represent women in sports and the "run, jane, run" marathon, which was created by the Fort Wayne Women's Bureau and is now a national event. The universal symbol for woman is used as a quilting motif throughout.

The corners of the quilt show the initials of the organization, "FWWB," and the years, "1976" and "1986." Leaving nothing undone, Mary Leggitt, head of the volunteers, embroidered the quilters' names in a sunburst design on the back. The quiltmakers were: Ardis Behrendt, Margaret Boerger, Inez Brownfield, Bernice Enyeart, Jean Fairman, Carole Gordon, Anna Kajuch, Jennifer Lawburgh, H. "Sue" McCullough, Liddy Parsons, Carol Ann Pickering, Martha Pohl, Ann Richardson, Vivian G. Schmidt, Bonita Siders, Gretchen Wiegel, and Marty Wyall. The quilting was finished by Joyce DeHaven of Churubusco. The quilt hangs in the Women's Bureau of Fort Wayne.

The Women's Bureau has programs dealing with rape awareness, peer counseling, self-defense, home repairs, single parenting, and teen parenting, and offers training services for women in transition and displaced homemakers.

"A Celebration of Womanhood"

Tenth Anniversary Quilt. Appliqued. Original design by Alison R. Adams. Executed by volunteers.
Fort Wayne, Allen County, Indiana. 1986. Cotton. 90" × 88".
Collection of the Fort Wayne Women's Bureau.

Amish Quilts

Rolling Stone. Family name, Jonnie Around the Corner. Pieced quilt. Made by Goldie O'Niel-Eash Christner. Topeka, LaGrange County, Indiana. Circa 1930. Cotton. 80" × 64½". Collection of Sue Christner.

Indiana is home to a large Amish population, and, although they are scattered throughout the state, the largest concentration is in northeastern Indiana. The Amish have produced some of the most extraordinary of all quilts. Amish quilts are easily identified by their styles and colors.

Amish quiltmakers used a simple geometric patchwork pattern, often with black or another dark color as the dominant fabric, and added bright plain colors, usually scraps left over from clothing. The result is a quilt with a contemporary feel and a graphic visual effect. Quilts like the two shown here are typical of those produced before 1940 and are being made today only on demand. Today Amish quiltmakers are being influenced by the world outside their communities. There is a large market for

Bear Paw. Pieced quilt. Maker unknown. Probably Plevna, Howard County, Indiana. Circa 1920. Cotton. 80" × 66½". Collection of Charlotte Armstrong.

Amish quilts today, and this market has dictated size, pattern, and fabric selection.

The Rolling Stone quilt depicted here is especially striking, with bold, bright colors and simple geometric shapes. An elaborate cable pattern used in the border quilting offers a strong contrast. The typical Amish quiltmaker is not concerned about placing all her fabrics in the same direction, as is evident in the Bear Paw quilt. Only two colors are used, but they show distinct variations that help to create the "sparkle." The quilting designs—pumpkin seeds, scrolls, and cables—add to the interest.

The Indiana State Museum houses the largest collection of quilts from the Indiana Amish in the United States.

Acknowledgments

The Indiana Quilt Registry Project, Inc., is indebted to many people and organizations for their support and generosity:

The quiltmakers of the past, who left behind a legacy for our discovery and enjoyment.

The quilt owners who entrusted their precious heirlooms and family memories to IQRP for archival documentation and exhibition, and who shared the family photographs used in this publication.

Those individuals and groups who have encouraged the efforts of IQRP with paid memberships and the financing of Registry Days.

The Indiana State Museum for their continuous support, for hosting our exhibition, and for the care and keeping of IQRP archival materials.

The Indiana University Press for publishing this book.

The Indiana Arts Commission and the National Endowment for the Arts for generous supporting grants for the 1987 Fabric Dating Workshop, documentation expense, computer input expense, and funding the color photography for this publication.

The Cummins Engine Company for grants matching monies raised for the Columbus and Madison Registry Days.

Mr. and Mrs. Wilbur Meese for their generous donation and the Eli Lilly Company Foundation for their employee-double-matching grant.

The National Quilting Association for their grant, used to copy the family photographs used in this book.

Cuesta Benberry, quilt historian, for writing the story of Marie Webster.

Niloo Paydar, Curator of Textiles, and the Archives of the Indianapolis Museum of Art for the photograph of Marie Webster.

Nancy Bryk, Curator of Domestic Life, and the Archives of the Henry Ford Museum for the photographs of Susan McCord and her quilt.

Don Distel of Spahr Photography for the color photography.

Steve and Sylvia Happe of Creative Arts for their work copying the family photographs used in this book.

Katy Christopherson of the Kentucky Quilt Project for her valuable assistance in getting the project started; Nancy Hewison, Purdue University librarian, for her contributions; and Dorothy Stites Alig for information on the conservation and care of textiles.

And especially the volunteers, those wonderful people who came through again and again, at Registry Days throughout the state, to accomplish the work involved, and who became staunch supporters and friends.

Members of the Indiana Quilt Registry Project

R. Emma Abroham
Sharolyn Hicks Ackelmire
Dora Aldred
Peg Alexander
Dorothy Stites Alig
Ilah Allsop
Mrs. Gene Anderson
Dianne Andrews
Theodora Andrews
B. J. Armbruster
Corinne Arthur
Ruth Aschleman
Delores Ashpaugh

Mary Jane Baker
Ruth L. Baker
Jennifer Bail
Sami A. Bailey
R. Andrea Barber
Josephine Barrow
D. Elaine Baumgardt
Chris Beldin
Nancy Bickmore
Edna Bierrum
Carla Black
Janet Blickenstaff
Penny A. Bloemker
Judith Winther Blosser
Bessie Richardson Boone
Judy Borron
Phyllis M. Borton
Jane P. Bottorff

Kathern D. Boyce
Ann Boyer
Betty Brandon
Loiseen Brewer
Linda R. Brewster
Bernard A. Bridges
Janis Broderick
Sandra Brooks
Doris M. Brothers
Mary Sue Brown
Janice Buffington
Clarene Bugher
Avis Burge
Ami C. Burkhart
Delora A. Burkhart
Ned Bush

Irene Campbell
Vicki Carlson
Ruby K. Carter
Catherine Carvey
Joanne Casey
Cass County Historical Society
June Cero
Ruth Chrena
Sue Christner
Katy Christopherson
B. Marlene Clary
Alma Clendenin
Columbus Star Quilters of
    Columbus
Bertha J. Conrad

Mrs. James W. Cook
Linda L. Copas
Hope S. Copeland
Xenia Cord
Rebie Crager
Virginia Craig
Ann Miller Crispin
Juanita Crowl
Mary Glenn Cullison
Mary Curry

Dinah Dalder
Joan M. Dart
Christopher Day
Christine Deitchley
Annette DeLaCroix
Kent DeLaCroix
Willodene Dillon
Carol Dodson
Bobbi Doll
Elizabeth Doss
Nancy Dowhower
Mary Ann Drahman
Mary Drook
Mollie Dudgeon
Joan Dugan
Ruth Dunker

Patricia Engelland
Evening Quilters Guild of
    Muncie

Georgia Lee Farr
Mrs. Charles Farris
Doris Farthing
Herbert B. Feldmann
Kenneth Fike
Roxanne Fike
Gladys Forgey
Esther Applegate Foster
Yvonne Frash
LaVera Friend
Friendly Persuasion Quilters
    of Vernon

Helen M. Gallett
Mary Galliher
Mildred L. Ganson
Wahneta Gebhart
Mildred Goins
Marilyn Goldman
Imogene Gooch
Delores A. Good
Sandy Gootee
Mary Alice Gorder
Judith A. Gordon
Gail Gorka
Sharon Gorup
Nancy C. Gray
Peggy M. Greene
Faye H. Groves
Mary Ann Guy
Carol J. Guytan

Mary Hagen
Carol Hall
Jenny Hall
Susan Handschy
Mary Ellen Handwork
N. Pearl Harbett
Harmony Quilters of
    Commiskey
Annette Harreld
Betsy Harris
Elizabeth J. Harrison
Louise L. Hartley
Virginia Hartsough
Sarah Hartzler
Karen Cochran Hasler
R. Hawthorne
Wanda Hayward
Carol Heckman
Martha Heidt
Nancy Hewison
Linda Hibner
Eleanor Hickman
Theresa Hinshaw
Joanna Hock
Neoma J. Hollenbaugh
Hoosier Heritage Quilt
    Guild of Lebanon
Mary Kay Horn
Mrs. Ralph Horner
Sue Huckstep
Martha Hudlow
Roberta Hunt

Mrs. William Ingle

Mary Jasheway
Mildred L. Jester
Johnson County Historical
    Society
Joyce Johnson
Phyllis R. Johnson
Mary E. Jones
Helen J. Julian

Nancy Kastner
Eva Jane Kelley
Pam Keltyka
Cedona Kendall
Frances R. Kepner
Marsha Kibbey
Frances P. Kilgore
Mary Kirk
Viola Kirkpatrick
Kathleen Klueber
Vickie Ko
Evelyn Kocher
Linda Koeneman
Beth Koenen-Seelbach
Pamela Koontz
Anita Hawkins Krug
Janet Kult

Lafayette American Sewing
    Guild of Lafayette
Susan Lambergtus
Jennifer Lawburgh
Edith Lawson
Millie Leathers
Vivian I. LeBeau
Gen Lehman
Maralee Lewis
Beverly Light
Susan Linson
Charlotte Lyle
Patricia Lyons

Carol Mackey
Hazel Marable
Louadda C. Marks
Susie Marvel
Jean Mathews
Treva May
Ruth McCammon
Evelyn DePue McClure
Marie McCorkle
Mrs. Jacob McDonnell
Patricia Ann McGuire
Kathleen McLary
Jean Meese
Leona Mendenhall
Beatrice Miller
Beatrice M. Miller
Gayle Miller
Kathy L. Miller
Rosalind Mitchel
Barbara Mitchell
Martha Modesitt
Janet C. Moeller
Dorothy S. Moore
Marian Moore
Regina M. Moore
Judy Morton
Mary E. Morton
Muncie Quilters Guild of
    Muncie
Cathi Myers
Janet Myers
Wilma Jeanne Myers

Elizabeth C. Nesbitt
Elsie A. Nickel
Marion Nicksich

Old Tippecanoe Quilt
    Guild of West Lafayette
Lori Overdorf

Marilyn Patterson
Ellen Penwell
Mary G. Persyn
Mary L. Peters
Nora K. Phillips
Rose Pierce
Betty Plant

Judith B. Pleiss
Wilma M. Plotner
Judy H. Poor
Peggy L. Potts
Harriet Powlen-Slaughter
Marilyn Prather
Beverly J. Price
Kathern Pruitt
Cecelia A. Purciful
Judith E. Purgason

Quilters Guild of Indianapolis

Deborah Raines
Raintree Quilters Guild of
    Newburgh
Anna L. Rardon
LaDonna Ratcliff
Mercedes Ratliff
Redbud Quilt Guild of
    Anderson
Diane Redlarczyk
Kathee Reed
Linda Regelean
Virginia Reklis
Anita Reynolds
Jan Reynolds
Alice P. Rinard
Mary F. Rinne
Nanilee Robarge
Georgia A. Roberts
Helen Rose
Marilyn Rosenbaum
Helen Roth
Judith L. Runyan

Susan Sanderock
Anne Scales
Mary Elizabeth Schaller
Georgiana Schroeder
Jane M. Schuett
Caryl Schuetz
Julia Schulz
Marjorie Schwier
Norma Seal
Marjorie Sears
Linda Shaffer
Mrs. C. R. Shell
Christina F. Shenberger
Kathy A. Shields
Clara Short
Mary Ann Showalter
Diane Siddens
Bonita Siders
Mary-Jo Sidewell-Murphy
Gayle L. Simriga
Ann L. Skene
Jeanette Skwarcan
Debra Smith
Julie Smith
Marcella B. Smith
Martha Smith

Mildred Smolek
Mary E. Soper
Jane Speck
Cheryl A. Spence
Spring Valley Quilt Guild
    of Pendleton
Victorena Stanis
Ginna Stanley
Alice Jo Star
Becky Steinmetz
Alice Stewart
Mary E. Stewart
Rosemary A. Stockwell
Diane E. Stott
Chris Stubblefield
Carole Sutton
Judy Sweeney

Hannah M. Taylor
Judy Mercer Tescher
Marilyn Tolhulzen

Arlowa Vorm

Virginia H. Wagner
LaVonne Waldron
Naomi Walker
Pat Ward
Carol Warner
Betty L. Warren
Mary M. Waters
Letha M. Wehrle
Virginia Weiss
Jacquolyne Werner
Kaye Greer West
Roberta Westfall
Sylvia Whitesides
Marguerite Wiebusch
Richard Wiebusch
Rita Willingham
Lauren M. Winger
Gretchen Winkleman
June Wolpert
Dr. P. J. Wood
Marlene Woodfield
Gail Reid Woodruff
Mrs. James B. Wright

Lina M. Zerkle

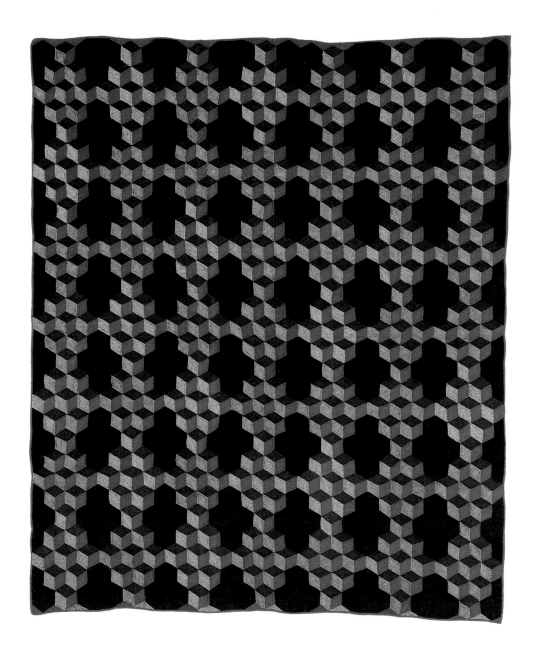

Hattie's Wool Baby Blocks

Baby Blocks. Also called Tumbling Blocks. Made by Hattie Beardsley Montgomery.
Owensville, Gibson County, Indiana. 1920, dated on the quilt. Wool. 82½″ × 65¾″.
Collection of Evadean Gordon.

This dazzling version of the Baby Blocks pattern was hand-pieced from red, black, and blue wool scraps cut into diamonds and hexagons. Dark brown quilting thread was used for outline quilting in the blocks and cross-hatch quilting in the black areas. The backing is red flannel.

According to the family, Hattie Beardsley Montgomery (1863–1959), a housewife with three children, made the quilt for utilitarian reasons; the bedrooms in her house were unheated at the time. On the back of her quilt, Hattie embroidered "HM 1920." It eventually was a gift to her grandson.

Research Site History

The following is the historical record of the research sites of the Indiana Quilt Registry Project. They are listed by date, city, site place, chairman, sponsoring groups, and number of quilts registered.

1. April 11, 1987: Vincennes, Green Auditorium. Judy Morton. Daughters of the American Revolution. 122 quilts

2. May 23, 1987: Anderson, Senior Citizens Center. Anne Scales. Redbud Quilt Guild. 237 quilts

3. July 14, 1987: Auburn, United Methodist Church. Roxanne Fike. Spinning Spools Quilt Guild. 237 quilts

4. August 15, 1987: Terre Haute, South Vigo High School. Peggy Potts, Pat Engelland, and Marlene Clary. Vigo County Historical Society, Vigo County Quilters Guild, Swope Art Alliance, YWCA, DAR, Women's Department Club, and Quilts 'n' More Shop. 483 quilts

5. October 3, 1987: Merrillville, Harrison Junior High School. Carol Brownewell. Heritage Quilt Club of Crown Point. 447 quilts

6. November 7, 1987: Lafayette, Christ United Methodist Church. Anita Hawkins Krug. Old Tippecanoe Quilt Guild. Tippecanoe County Extension Homemakers. 239 quilts.

7. December 5, 1987: Wabash, Honeywell Center. Nancy Jacoby. Nancy J's Fabrics. 243 quilts

8. January 12, 1988: Indiana State Museum collection. Kathleen McLary. IQRP board. 22 quilts

9. March 5, 1988: Bloomington, St. Paul's United Methodist Church. Regina Moore. Bloomington Quilt Guild. 481 quilts

10. March 21, 1988: Lafayette, Tippecanoe County Historical Association. Anita Hawkins Krug. Old Tippecanoe Quilt Guild. 24 quilts

11. April 9, 1988: Columbus, Donner Center. Janice Sefton Foss. Columbus Star Quilters. 294 quilts

12. May 16, 1988: Dearborn, Mi., Henry Ford Museum. Marilyn Goldman. 10 quilts

13. May 21, 1988: South Bend, Indiana University, South Bend Campus. Yvonne Frash. The River Bend Quilters, Quilts 'n' More Fabric Shop. Northern Indiana Historical Society. 385 quilts

14. June 25, 1988: Indianapolis, Pike High School. Mary Kay Horn. Quilters Guild of Indianapolis. 329 quilts

15. July 16, 1988: Evansville, University of Southern Indiana. Joanne Donahue. Raintree Quilters Guild. 223 quilts

16. August 13, 1988: Madison, National Guard Armory. Millie Leathers. Friendly Persuasion Quilters. 162 quilts

17. September 17, 1988: Connersville, UAW Local 151 Union Hall. Bev Houseman. IQRP Board. 68 quilts

18. October 15, 1988: Warsaw, First United Presbyterian Church. Ruth Dunker. Lakeland Quilt Club. 320 quilts

19. November 5, 1988: Greenwood, Greenwood Christian Church. Karen Cochran Hasler. Quilt Connection Quilt Guild, Johnson County Extension Homemakers, Johnson County Historical Society. 480 quilts

20. February 25, 1989: Valparaiso, Banta Senior Center. Kathy Phillips. String-A-Long Quilters. 347 quilts

21. March 4, 1989: Lebanon, Boone County 4-H Fairgrounds. Anita Hardwick. Hoosier Heritage Quilt Guild and Chat 'n' Do Home Economics Club. 374 quilts

22. April 8, 1989: Muncie, Minnetrista Cultural Center. Marilyn Goldman. Muncie Quilters Guild. 885 quilts

23. June 13, 1989. Indianapolis, Children's Museum. Marguerite Wiebusch. IQRP Board. 56 quilts

Ocean Waves Quilt

Ocean Waves. Pieced quilt. Maker unknown. Probably Blackford County, Indiana. Circa 1875.
Cotton. 79" × 62". Collection of Beth Gonser.

The Ocean Waves pattern was usually pieced in a block-to-block set; this unusual quilt is done with sashing between the twenty pieced blocks and is a scrap-bag encyclopedia of fabrics from the 1875 era.

Prints, plaids, stripes, checks, and dots have been combined in the blue, red, and yellow color scheme. The quilting was done diagonally, with ten stitches to the inch.

Volunteers

Judy Abbott
Jean Alsip
Carla Anderson
Debbie Anderson
Patricia Anderson
Susan Anderson
Dianne Andrews
*Anna Andrick
Ethel Anson
Pat Anson
Margaret Applegate
Charlotte Armstrong
Corinne Arthur
*Ruth Aschleman
*Delores Ashpaugh
Celia Auster
Edward Austin

*Cathy Bahnsen
Carol Bailey
Sami Bailey
Bonnie Baker
Gladys Baker
Malinda Baker
Margaret Baker
Lorrene Baldwin
Beverly Banselbach
Pamela Banta
Ellyn Barcus
Susan Barna
Irene Barnard
Edith Barnes

Julie Barnes
Ann Barnett
Ursel Bartley
Mary Beaver
Mary Jo Bennett
Darlene Beranek
Eileen Biagi
Karen Blaisdell
Kathy Blake
Janet Blickenstaff
Judith Blosser
Vickie Bonfiglio
Bessie Boone
Nancy Borth
Lynn Bosse
Ginny Bouchie
Phyllis Bousman
Ann Boyer
Barbara Boyer
Cynthia Boyer
*Ben Boyles
*Patricia Boyles
Betty Brandon
Diane Breman
Loiseen Brewer
Josephine Bridwell
Christine Bridy
Guinevere Brisbin
Dannel Brooks
*Sandy Brooks
Doris Brothers
Laura Brown

Maxine Brown
Peggy Brown
Carol Brownewell
Mary Lou Bruns
Nancy Bryk
Ruthann Bubp
Ruth Buckley
Linda Bucklin
Jan Buffington
Anne Bunch
Elizabeth Burcham
Avis Burge
Celeste Burgeson
Kathleen Burke
Sharon Burns
Shelley Burns
Betty Busald
Linda Bushman
Christine Butterfield
Dovie Byers

Donna Cambra
Donna Campbell
Victoria Carlson
Eva Case
Cleita Chambers
Pat Chance
Elizabeth Chaneske
Mike Chaneske
Elaine Chase
Delphine Childers
Sue Childes

Ruth Chrena
Sue Christner
Carol Clark
Irene Clarke
Marlene Clary
Jan Clayton
Sharon Clem
Marge Clements
Russ Clements
Alma Clendevin
Barbara Clifford
Milly Clifford
Sharon Clymer
Myrtle Coates
Wilma Coffman
Aleen Cole
Debbie Collins
Jolly Conrad
Mary Alice Cook
Millie Cook
Linda Copas
Myrna Cowger
Martha Cox
Jennie Craig
Eileen Crain
Lorraine Crandall
*Ann Crispin
Cathy Crowder
Kay Crowder
Mildred Cruser
Honore Cummings
Kathy Cunningham

*Worked three or more IQRP Registry Days

168

Celia Custer
Katrina Custer
Pat Cutshall

Barbara Daily
Dinah Dalder
Leah Dale
*Joan Dart
Sue Davis
Trish Deal
Helen Deig
Christine Deitchley
*Annette DeLaCroix
*Beulah DeLaCroix
*Kent DeLaCroix
Mary Alice DeLong
Lynn Demaree
Susan Deraner
Rachel Diamond
Louise Dickerson
Maryann Dietrich
Anne Dimit
Alice Dobson
*Carol Dodson
Joan Donahue
Norma Dougherty
Millie Dover
Connie Downey
*Mary Ann Drahman
Mary Drook
Celestra Drysdale
Ruby Duffalo

Joan Dugan
Jane Dunham
*Ruth Dunker
Joyce Dunn
Kathy Dunn-Child
Darlene Durbin
Joyce Durilet
Phyllis Durnal
Terry Dye

June Eaton
Wilma Jean Edwards
Connie Egli
Tracy Ehrhardt
Julie Eickhoff
Mary Louise Elder
Shirley Eller
Sandra Elliott
Peggy Engelbach
Patricia Engelland
Kathy Erickson
Cheryl Erskine
Laurel Everest
Carol Everman
Mary Evers

Betty Fager
Lucile Failing
Ann Fairhurst
Elizabeth Fallwell
Doris Farthing
Ruth Fauver

Susan Feninger
Lenora Festa
Andy Fike
*Ken Fike
*Roxanne Fike
Carolyn Finkenbinder
Ruth Finney
Sally Fish
Megan Fisher
Janet Fliger
Gladys Forgey
*Janice Foss
Donna Foy
Vonnie Frash
Karen Frazier
Jennie Freund
Aline Friedrick
LeVera Friend
Andrea Fry
Pamela Fuchs
Michal Fuller

*Mary Galliher
Mildred Ganson
Doris Garfinkel
Sharon Garman
*Marie Garrity
*Wahneta Gebhart
Betty Gerligs
Mary Geyer
Deanna Giles
Billie Gilmore

Jeannie Givens
Linda Glaze
Cleo Glecker
Margaret Glecker
Elaine Glover
Mary Gloyeske
Mildred Goins
*Marilyn Goldman
Beth Gonser
Imogene Gooch
Delores Good
Sally Goodin
Ethel Goodwin
Rose Goodwin
Betty Gordon
Beverly Gore
Ida Goss
Nancy Gray
*Peggy Greene
Charlotte Gridley
Lois Griffith
Catherine Groves
Paula Guffey
Carol Gutyan
Mary Ann Guy

Donna Hagan
Charles Hagen
Marilee Hagen
Mary Hagen
Doris Haggard
Dorothy Hahn

Vera Hakes
Carol Hall
Roseanna Halseman
Hilda Halsey
Virginia Hamilton
Loretha Hamke
Betty Hamman
Doris Hamman
Suann Handschy
Mary Ellen Handwork
Margaret Handy
Christen Hankin
Mary Ann Harbaugh
Anita Hardwick
Rita Harrington
Betsy Harris
David Harris
Ethel Harris
Barbara Hart
Anna Mae Hartsock
Sarah Hartzler
Martha Harvey
Mary Lou Harvey
*Karen Cochran Hasler
Mary Hasty
*Eleanor Haupt
Christine Hawkin
Colleen Hawkins
Pauline Heagy
Carol Heckman
Thais Heinzerling
Marcella Heldman
Avenal Heminger
Shirley Hendricks
Shelia Herman
Virginia Hess
Mary Lou Hessey
Nancy Hewison
Freda Hewitt
Kathleen Hiatt
Eleanor Hickman
Mary Ellen Hickman
Kathy Hicks
Carolyn Hines
Marlene Hirsch
Carol Hoffer
Pauline Holman
Alice Hoover
Debbie Horn
Kimberly Horn
*Mary Kay Horn
*Ralph Horn
Donella Horner
Hedy Horvath
Alice Hottenstein
Evaline Hour
Bev Houseman
Jane Howard
Von Howard
Eve Howes
Mary Hreha
Sue Huckstep

Martha Hudlow
Susan Hughes
Viola Hughes
Jean Hull
Mildred Hunter
Marceil Hutchison

Gwendolyn Isaac

Linda Jack
Ollie Jackson
Nancy Jacoby
Kathy Jarrett
Laura Jasheway
Mary Jasheway
Audrey Jay
Pat Jeelecoe
Annie Johnson
Dorothy Johnson
Eva Johnson
Joyce Johnson
Phyllis Johnson
Shirley Johnson
Bettye Jones
Loretta Jones
Wanetta Jones
Helen Jordan
Marjorie Joyner

Katie Kamm
Laura Kantzer
Paula Karmire
Glenda Kelley
Lillian Kelley
Helen Kelso
*Pamela Kennedy
Harriet Kennon
Mary Kerns
Barbara Kilgore
Nola King
Priscilla Kinney
Joann Kinser
Marian Kintz
Pat Kirby
Meg Kish
Kathie Klueber
Diana Knezevich
Diana Knezwick
Jan Knight
*Evelyn Kocher
Irene Kocher
Linda Koeneman
Beth Koenen-Seelbach
Jeff Kopkey
*Anita Hawkins Krug
LaVerda Krull
Dorothy Kuehl

Holly Labore
Helen LaFollette
Vinette Landers
Vera Lannerd

Myra Lantz
Gail Larsen
Cheryl Larson
Kandye Lawler
Edith Lawson
LuAnn Layman
*Millie Leathers
Vivian LeBeau
Pauline Lee
Genevieve Lehman
Pat Lehnen
Mary Lou Lemboke
Jeannie Leo
Allison Leopold
Janet Levihn
Maralee Lewis
Shirley Liby
Beverly Light
Mary Lillyblade
Susan Linson
Emilie Liston
Josephine Little
Elaine Locke
Billie Jo Loos
Linda Lorenz
Helen Loughmiller
Marti Lowery
Tanya Luce
Dorcas Luecke
Mary Lumm
Dorothy Lutes
Geraldine Lutz
Judith Luzadder
Charlotte Lyle
P. L. Lyons
Pat Lyons

Carol Mackey
Donna Macy
Pearl Mailath
Cynthia Majchrowicz
Anita Majeske
Joan Manning
Beverly Maresh
Louadda Marks
Dee Marquam
Hilda Marshall
Martha Martin
Sue Martin
Susie Marvel
Betty Ellen Mather
Jean Mathews
Pat Mathias
Mary Maxey
Edith May
Wathena Mayfield
Julie McCann
Evelyn McClure
Sherry McConnell
Shirley McConnell
Marie McCorkle
Victory McCullough

Eleanor McDade
Joan McDonald
Mary McGhee
Joan McGinnis
Dorothy McKay
*Kathleen McLary
Kate McNair
Claris Meeks
Helen Meharry
Leona Mendenhall
Mary Lynne Meranda
Betty Merz
Charmaine Meyer
Esther Michael
Beatrice Miller
Emily Miller
Gayle Miller
Helen Miller
Jane Miller
Sonda Miller
Janet Minch
Joe Mitchell
Kate Mitchell
Jane Moersch
Felicia Moody
Anne Moore
Jean Moore
*Regina Moore
Teresa Moore
Josephine Moorehead
Dorothy Morgan
Becky Morris
Sally Morrison
Judy Morton
Jacqueline Moster
Sally Moulton
Cathi Myers
Clifford Myers
*Janet Myers
Margaret Myers
Wilma Myers

Gwen Nabrey
Kathleen Naegeley
Lana Neal-Clark
Mona Nichols

Joan Owen

Franchion Pacmiter
Jane Padgett
Brenda Papadakis
Phyllis Payton
Beverly Pearce
Ruth Pedevilla
Vaughn Peebles
Susie Pelkey
*Ellen Penwell
Margaret Percifield
Alice Person
Mary Persyn
Rosemary Peterman

Sally Peters
Esther Pfluderer
Phyllis Philips
Kathy Phillips
Lola Phillips
Nora Phillips
Elizabeth Pidany
Judy Pleiss
*Wilma Plotner
Helen Pomenoy
Missy Ponko
Shirley Portolese
Lottie Potters
Cathy Potts
Peggy Potts
Janet Powers
Patty Prince
Cecelia Purciful

Susan Quandt
Ruth Quillen
Dorothy Quinlan
Henie Quintana

Debbie Raines
Lisa Rance
Gailanna Ransom
Rochelle Ransom
Rolissa Ransom
Doris Rasson
Mercedes Ratliff
Mary Rausch
B. J. Rayburn
Gwendolyn Reagan
Dinne Redlaiczuk
David Reece
Judi Reece
Linda Regelean
Elizabeth Renbarger
Gertie Reynolds
Emily Rich
Sara Rich
Beth Anne Rigney
Avanelle Rippey
Janet Ritzline
Nan Robarge
Dawn Roberts
Maurine Roehm
Garnet Roesel
Dory Rogers
Sandy Rogers
Cathy Roler
Marty Roman
Helen Rose
Martha Roso
Ruth Ross
Doris Rosson
Deanna Roudebush
Barbara Rush
Carol Russell
Erma Ryan

Linda Sage
Phyllis Said
Shirley Salway
Jim Sanders
Kathy Saunders
Anne Sayers
*Anne Scales
Jamie Schantz
Veronica Schlosser
Karen Schmidt
Alyce Schnelker
Mary Schnezzan
Anne Schnure
Rae Schroeder
Jane Schuett
Caryl Schuetz
Norma Jean Schwindy
Cleo Seaman
Louise Sellers
Maribelle Severine
Marge Sharan
Joanna Shearer
Marcia Sherrell
Beth Shiltz
Stacy Shopp
Inez Shoudy
Joan Shufran
Dianne Siddens
*Bonita Siders
Nila Sink
Jeanette Skawarcan
Kity Skelly
Vera Slack
Emma Lee Slagle
Rita Slankard
Abby Smith
Bernadine Smith
Charlotte Smith
*Debbie Smith
Kim Smith
Marcella Smith
Mary Smith
Sherry Smith
Mildred Smolick
Gayle Smriga
Helen Snyder
Cindy Sochan
Faye Sosbe
Elberetta Souther
Roberta Sowers
Janet Spears
Ruth Speer
Mary Spell
*Cheryl A. Spence
Betty Spencer
Betty Speth
Ronda Staekey
Victorena Stanis
Ginna Stanley
Jan Stapp
Alice Star
Wilma Steckel

Edna Steffey
Judith Stein
Barbara Stephan
Beth Stepp
Erin Stepp
Catherine Steppe
Patricia Steward
Thelma Steward
Helen Stingley
Normajean Stone
Sue Striggle
Barbara Stringfield
Adeline Stuckey
Ellen Stuckey
Thelma Summers
Mary Summit
Pam Sutherland
Judy Sweeney
Marie Swofford
Jean Szymanski

Helene Talen
Arthur Tavern
Mary Tawney
Martha Taylor
Peggy Taylor
Mary Jane Teeters-Eichacker
Judy Tescher
Roseanna Thalsema
Marilyn Thompson
Catherine Thurin
Mary Jane Todd
Marilyn Tolhuizen
Janna Toney
Nannette Triplette
Rosemary Trubitt
Gail Tschida
Deanna Turner
Linda Turner

Marge Ullery
Clara Uzelac

Sara VanBuskirk
Harlean VanNess
Betty Vehslage
Theresa Veldman
Diana Venters
Janet Von Holt

Lynn Wade
Charlotte Wagner
Jessie Wainscott
LaVonne Waldron
Christine Walker
Mary Walker
Mary Beth Walter
Pat Walters
Marge Wasmer
Pam Wasmer
Mary Waters
Ruth Ann Waters

Marianne Watson
Patricia Watson
Ruth Ann Watson
Virginia Weiss
Elizabeth Weller
Jacquelyne Wemb
Doris Werner
Jacquolyne Werner
Roberta Westfall
Mary Gladys Wheeler
Jean White
*Sylvia Whitesides
*Marguerite Wiebusch
Richard Wiebusch
Jane Wienham
Leonora Wiggins
Jane Wilhelm
Claudia Wilkes
Frances Williams
Margaret Williams
Marian Williams
Rita Willingham
Lesley Wilson
Libby Wilson
Judy Wink
Gretchen Winkleman
Belle Winter
Margaret Wire
Sandy Witt
Anne Woftas
*June Wolpert
Anne Wood
Helen Wood
*Dr. P. J. Wood
Marlene Woodfield
Diana Woodward
Jeannette Woodworth
Kathryn Woolridge
Mary Wray
Betty Wright
JoAnn Wright
Laurel Wright
Mary Wright
Sheila Wright
Mary Ann Wunder

Frances Young

Louise Zahn
Lina Zerkle
Ercell Zink

Quilts of Indiana: Crossroads of Memories Book Committee, shown with their "Tribute to the Indiana Rose" quilt. Seated, Cheryl A. Spence, Mary Kay Horn, Karen Cochran Hasler. Standing, Marguerite Kersey Wiebusch, Roxanne Fike, Kathleen McLary, Anita Hawkins Krug, and Marilyn Goldman. Not pictured, Anne Scales.

IQRP Board Members

ROXANNE FIKE: Registry Site Photographer, Book Committee

MARILYN GOLDMAN: Co-Chairperson Book Committee, IQRP Secretary, IQRP Newsletter Editor, Exhibit Committee

KAREN COCHRAN HASLER: Chairperson Public Relations, Chairperson of Education, Book Committee, Exhibit Committee

MARY KAY HORN: Registry Site Photographer, IQRP Quilt Designer, Book Committee, Exhibit Committee

ANITA HAWKINS KRUG: IQRP Vice-Chairperson, Chairperson of Membership, Education Committee, Funding Committee, Book Committee, Exhibit Committee

MILLIE LEATHERS: Member Board of Directors

KATHLEEN McLARY: IQRP Chairperson, Chairperson Exhibit Committee, Funding Committee, Book Committee

ELLEN PENWELL: IQRP Vice Chairperson, Chairperson Funding Committee

ANNE SCALES: Chairperson Registry Sites, Book Committee

CHERYL A. SPENCE: IQRP Treasurer, Membership Committee, Funding Committee, Book Committee, Exhibit Committee

MARGUERITE WIEBUSCH: Co-Chairperson Book Committee, Chairperson Documentation, IQRP Logo Designer, Exhibit Committee

Others serving on the Board of Directors during the project were: Delores Ashpaugh, Sandy Brooks, Judy Morton, Jan Reynolds, and Bonita Siders.

Dewey's Little Quilt. Pattern also called Hummingbird. Pieced and quilted by Dewey Fisher. Circa 1950. Martin County, Indiana. Cotton. 28½" × 21". Collection of Shirley Ewick.

Aquilt may be made for many reasons. Often it is a gift for someone who occupies an especially warm spot in the heart of the quiltmaker. Shirley Ewick's father had an old friend named Dewey Fisher—a lifelong bachelor whose only family was his dog. As a farmer, Dewey was used to hard work, but his hobby was doing many kinds of needlework, including quilting and crocheting. Using scraps from his old clothes, he made several small quilts for his pet dog and another for Shirley's father's dog. Dewey is still remembered by Shirley's family because of this quilt.

Glossary and Standards

All-over quilting design—A quilting motif used over the entire surface of the quilt regardless of the pieced or appliqued design. Rainbow quilting, clamshell, diamonds, and parallel lines are examples.

Alternate set—Pieced and/or appliqued blocks placed next to blocks of plain fabric.

Altered quilt—The changed quilt may have been cut down in size, have corners cut out, or have edges and/or borders trimmed. Bindings and/or borders may also have been replaced. Check for distortions in the pattern and non-matching fabrics, especially fabrics of a much later vintage. Old tops that have been newly quilted. Old blocks made into a new top.

Applique—Construction technique of applying fabric to a backing using stitches such as buttonhole, blind stitch, or whip stitch.

Bar set—Strips of fabric set together lengthwise. May be whole cloth, pieced or appliqued, such as in Amish Bars, Flying Geese, or Tree Everlasting. Sometimes called Bands.

Batt—A type of filler used between the quilt top and quilt back. May be cotton, polyester, wool, or silk. Raw cotton batt usually contains debris from the cotton plant pod and stalk and is called "cotton seeds"—a misnomer, but part of the popular vernacular.

Binding—Edge treatment. Types of applied binding may include woven tape, braid, ribbon, lace, etc.

Block repeat—Use of the same block design, either identical or by mixing colors, to create a quilt top.

Border—Fabric framework for the block area or medallion area of the quilt. Edge to which binding is attached.

Broderie perse—Chintz fabric designs cut out and appliqued to whole cloth. Most popular in late eighteenth and early nineteenth century quilts. Also called cut-out chintz quilts.

Calico—Popular weight and type of cotton fabric usually in colors and with small figures on the ground.

Chintz—A glazed cotton fabric. May be printed with elaborate motifs of flowers, fruit, trees, and birds.

Comfort—Product consisting of a top, batt or filler, and backing fabric held together by tying or tacking at intervals. Ties may be yarn or thread. Also called a comfortable or comforter.

Corded quilting—Parallel lines are quilted and a cord or piece of yarn is threaded into the channel from the back. Frequently seen with stuffed work or trapunto.

Cotton/poly fabric—Fabric which is at least 50% cotton. Used in quilts since the 1960s.

Coverlet—Product which is woven on a loom, consisting of one or two layers and used as a bed covering.

Crazy, all-over—A quilt made on one large foundation piece with randomly shaped pieces added without a definite plan. Crazy quilts usually do not have a filler or stitches, but are tacked and embellished.

Crazy, contained—A type of crazy quilt with definite blocks, strips, or diamonds. Each individual section may be sewn in a "crazy" manner.

Cross-hatch quilting—Evenly spaced quilting lines which form squares horizontally and vertically. Commonly used as a fill-in or background design.

Crosspatch—Two or more geometric blocks combined to produce a coherent overall quilt design separate in identity from the individual blocks from which the design is composed.

Dye changes—Discoloration, splitting, or disintegrating in specific color areas of the fabric. Some greens fade to tan, or, in the case of an overdyed green, the blue color fades to expose the yellow or vice versa.

Echo or Hawaiian quilting—follows the outlines of the appliques for the first line of quilting, then makes concentric rows about ½" apart until the whole surface is covered.

Edge treatment—Using piping, prairie points, ruffles, or conventional applied binding, etc., to finish a quilt.

English piecing—Construction technique of basting fabric over a paper-shaped foundation in order to hold it and stitch it to an adjoining piece.

Feedsack—Coarsely woven cotton fabric, either patterned or plain, used to make bags for holding grain or household staples.

Filler—The substance used between the quilt top and quilt back.

Hanging-diamond quilting—Evenly spaced diagonal quilting lines which cross, forming diamonds. Commonly used as background or fill-in quilting.

Image content—What is shown on the quilt: people, faces, hands, animals, buildings, etc.

Inscriptions—Dedications, names, dates, places, Bible verses, etc., that may be quilted in, embroidered on, or penned upon the quilt. Look in the corners for initials or among the quilting stitches.

In-the-ditch quilting—Quilting stitches placed in the seam line where two pieces of fabric are joined.

Log cabin—A type of quilt block construction wherein strips of fabric are sewn together perpendicularly, sometimes utilizing a backing fabric.

Log cabin block variations—Starting with a base piece, which may be a square, rectangle, diamond, or hexagon, and which may be centered or offcenter, pieces of fabric (the logs) are added to form the quilt block. Variations are almost endless, but among the best known are Sunshine and Shadows, Courthouse Steps, Pineapple, and Chimneys and Cornerstones.

Log cabin quilt sets—These are the numerous choices for positioning the finished quilt blocks. Blocks constructed in the Sunshine and Shadows variation, for example, may be arranged as pinwheels, chevrons, straight lines of color, zigzags of light and dark, concentric squares, or X's. The Courthouse Steps variation may be placed with all lights side by side or alternating with light and dark colors.

Logo—A symbol or lettering, sometimes of a commercial firm, used for identification.

Meander quilting—Sometimes called free motion quilting. Lines of quilting on the surface of the quilt without a pre-set pattern.

Measurements—All measurements are in inches, using a steel tape. Length precedes width.

Medallion—A quilt top constructed of a large central block surrounded by borders. Construction may be a combination of techniques.

Muslin—Popular weight and type of cotton quilting material. Usually in bleached white or unbleached natural colors.

Novelty print—Any fabric with an outstanding or easily recognizable design. Examples are cartoon characters used in children's clothing.

Novelty quilt—Construction techniques other than pieced, appliqued, or whole cloth. Examples are yo-yos, cathedral windows, and biscuit quilts.

On point—Blocks placed on the diagonal and sewn together.

Outline quilting—Quilting ¼" from a seam line or appliqued shape.

Patchwork—The seaming together of planned pieces of fabrics, that will result in patterned blocks. The pieces may be straight or curved so long as they fit together into a pattern.

Pattern name—Name for the quilt design used by the owner, the maker, or used in reference. All three may be different.

Poly/cotton fabric—A blend of man-made polyester and natural cotton fibers, sometimes favored for their crease resistance and ability to hold their color. The blend is 50% or more polyester.

Prairie points—Folded fabric squares which when sewn to the edges of a quilt and pointed out make a decorative sawtooth finish in lieu of a normal binding. They can also appear elsewhere.

Premium—A small piece of fabric adorned with a picture or portrait, commercially printed or woven. These were sometimes given by companies as bonuses for buying their product. Other types may include fair ribbons, political insignia, logos or symbols of fraternal organizations, and religious motifs.

Pressed method—Construction technique used in Log Cabins and crazy quilts which utilizes a base or foundation fabric to which the strips or patches are sewn and no quilting is needed. The top is tacked or tied to the backing and filler if any.

Printed quilt—Fabric printed commercially to resemble traditional patchwork or applique designs and used as a quilt top or back as it is. Referred to as "cheater cloth."

Quadrant—A type of quilt top which can be visually divided into four equal sections.

Quilt—A product of three layers—a top, batting or filler, and a backing fabric held together with stitches.

Quilt-as-you-go—A technique by which the quilt blocks are sandwiched with the batting and backing and quilted as individual units prior to becoming part of the whole quilt.

Quilting thread—Strong thread used to permanently hold together three layers of fabric in a quilt. May be waxed for easier use.

Reference number—The archival number given each quilt by the IQRP. It consists of two block letters indicating the site at which it was registered, a hyphen, and three numbers for identification.

Reverse applique—Construction technique wherein a top layer of fabric is cut away to reveal another fabric layer underneath. The edges of the top fabric are turned under and sewn down.

Sampler—A quilt top with a variety of different block patterns. May be constructed with a combination of techniques.

Sashing—The fabric placed between the blocks. Sashing may be plain, pieced, and/or appliqued.

Sashing connecting blocks—Block placed where the vertical and horizontal sashings meet.

Seminole patchwork—Strips of fabric sewn together, then cut apart and reassembled to form a new geometric design.

Set—The manner in which quilt blocks are sewn together into a top.

Single template—One pattern piece, such as a square, triangle, hexagon, diamond, or rhombus, used to create an entire quilt top.

Stipple quilting—Quilting lines or patterns less than ⅛ inch apart in area.

Stitches per inch—In three separate places, the documenter counted the number of quilting stitches showing on the top surface of the quilt in an inch measurement.

Straight set—Quilt blocks sewn together side by side.

String piecing—A method of utilizing a random sewing of fabric strips to form a new piece of fabric from which pattern pieces may be cut.

Surface decoration—Decorative embroidery stitches or any kind of embellishment attached to the quilt.

Trapunto—Extra filler or stuffing placed in a quilted motif. After a design is quilted, the backing is opened and stuffing material is pushed into the opening, giving the motif a padded effect. Also called stuffed work or Italian quilting.

Up/down orientation—Visually the design has a top and bottom. The quilt is properly viewed from one direction.

Whole-cloth quilt—Can be all white, or any solid color, and may be two or more like pieces sewn together to make the whole. The quilting design executed upon the cloth composes the style of the quilt itself. It contains no patchwork, applique, or other embellishments, except possibly trapunto.

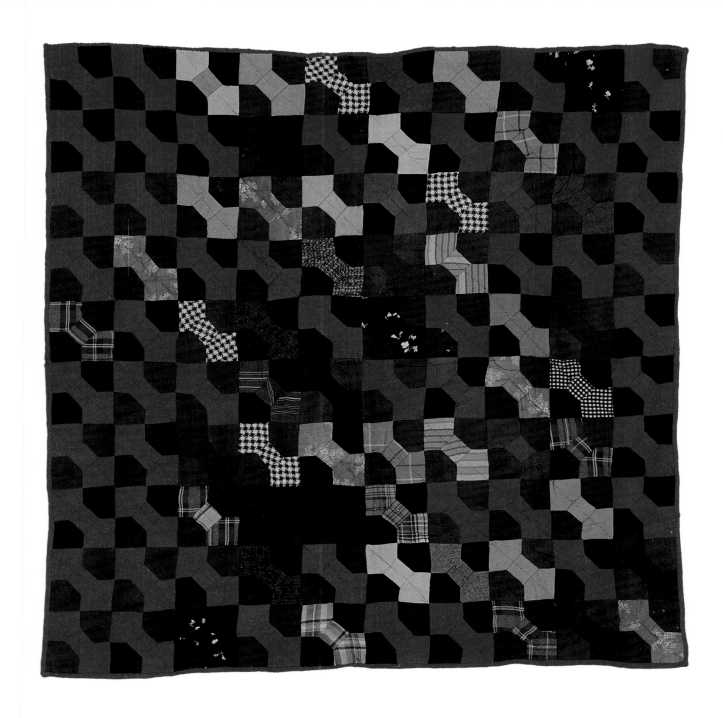

Bow Tie. Pieced quilt. Made by Laura Elizabeth Wolf Cooper. 1898. Orange County, Indiana. Wool and cotton. 40½" × 40". Collection of Ann McCasland.

This trundle bed quilt was originally made in 1898 by Laura Elizabeth Wolf Cooper of Orange County, Indiana, for Laura's granddaughter, Tina Felknor. It is now in the possession of the maker's great-granddaughter.

Bibliography

"An Encyclopedia of Pieced Quilt Patterns," compiled by Barbara Brackman. Lawrence: Kansas: Self-published, n.d.

Benberry, Cuesta, "Charm Quilts Revisited," Parts I and II. *Quilter's Newletter Magazine*, Nos. 198 (January 1988) and 199 (February 1988).

Beyer, Jinny. *The Scrap Look*. McLean, Virginia: EPM Publications, Inc. 1985.

Brackman, Barbara, *Clues in the Calico: A Guide to Identifying and Dating Antique Quilts*. McLean, Virginia: EPM Publications, Inc. 1989.

Brown, Genevieve, A. N. Bobbitt, and J. Otto Lee. *Indiana*. Indianapolis: Board of Public Printing, 1930.

Colby, Averil. *Quilting*. New York: Charles Scribner's Sons. 1971.

Dégh, Linda, ed. *Indiana Folklore, A Reader*. Bloomington: Indiana University Press, 1980.

Hall, Carrie A., and Rose G. Kretsinger, *The Romance of the Patchwork Quilt in America*. New York: Bonanza Books, 1935.

History of Grant County, Indiana. Chicago: Brant & Fuller, 1886.

Kemper, G. W. H., ed. *A Twentieth Century History of Delaware County, Indiana*, vol. 1. Chicago: Lewis Publishing Company, 1908.

Kirkpatrick, Ralph, Recordkeeper for the Back Creek Friends Meeting and area Quaker groups in Grant County. Interview.

Kunhardt, Dorothy Meserve, and Phillip B. Kunhardt, Jr. *Twenty Days*. Edition published by arrangement with Harper and Row, 1965.

Leman, Bonnie, and Judy Martin. *Log Cabin Quilts*. Wheatridge, Colorado: MQM Publishing Co. 1980.

Lesley, Martha A., and Pauline Brunton. *The History of Wea Township and the Wea Willing Workers*. 1974.

Marston, Gwen, and Joe Cunningham. *Sets and Borders*. Paducah, Kentucky: American Quilters Society. 1987.

Nylander, Jane C. *Fabrics for Historic Buildings: A Guide to Selecting Reproduction Fabrics*. Washington, D.C.: Preservation Press, 1983.

Pettit, Florence H. *America's Printed and Painted Fabrics, 1600–1900*. New York: Hastings House Publishers.

Pottinger, David. *Quilts from Indiana Amish*. New York: E. P. Dutton, Inc., 1983.

Putt, Dawne Lisa. "Lincoln Lore Sewn Up in Quilt," *Kokomo* (Indiana) *Tribune*. June 12, 1988.

Rehmel, Judy. *The Quilt I.D. Book*. New York: Prentice-Hall, 1986.

Safford, Carleton L., and Robert Bishop. *America's Quilts and Coverlets*. New York: E. P. Dutton, 1980.

Sasianow, Allen, Professor of History, Indiana University, Kokomo Campus. Telephone interview regarding KKK history.

Smith, Mildred, Americus Quilting Club Historian. Interview.

Spurgeon, Wiley W., Jr. *Muncie and Delaware County: An Illustrated Retrospective*. Woodland Hills, California: Windsor Publications, Inc., 1984.

Stringfellow, Dick, Curator of the Tippecanoe County Historical Association. Interviews.

Wabash County, Indiana, History. Bicentennial Commemorative Edition, 1976.

Webster, Marie D., *Quilts, Their Story and How to Make Them*. New York: Doubleday, Page and Company, 1915.

Wein, Carol Ann. *The Great American Log Cabin Quilt Book*. New York: E. P. Dutton, Inc. 1984.

Wheeler, Jesse H., Historian, United Methodist Church. *Quilts*. Dayton, Indiana: self-published, 1979.

Wilkinson, Ona and Rosalie. *The Wilkinson Art Quilt* (catalog). Ligonier, Indiana: Wilkinson Quilt Company, 1916.

Wilson, Marilyn L., *Annie's Quilt*, Vermont Northfield News and Printery, James and Ingrid Wilson, Publishers, 1987.

World Book Encyclopedia. Robert E. Million, Jr., on Indiana.

Index

Editor: ROBERTA L. DIEHL
Book and Jacket Designer: SHARON L. SKLAR
Production Coordinator: HARRIET CURRY
Typeface: CASLON 540/AVANT GARDE
Compositor: G&S TYPESETTERS, INC.
Printer: TOPPAN PRINTING CO.